1,500
LITERARY
REFERENCES
EVERYONE
SHOULD
KNOW

D0036219

1,500 LITERARY REFERENCES EVERYONE SHOULD KNOW

Lloyd T. Grosse
and
Alan F. Lyster

ARCO PUBLISHING, INC.
NEW YORK

Published by Arco Publishing, Inc.
215 Park Avenue South, New York, N.Y. 10003

Library of Congress Cataloging in Publication Data

Grosse, Lloyd T.
    1500 literary references everyone should know.

    1. Allusions—Dictionaries.   I. Lyster, Alan.
II. Title.   III. Title: One thousand five hundred
literary references everyone should know.
PN43.G66   1983   803   82-18444
ISBN 0-668-05596-0 (pbk.)

Printed in the United States of America

The authors wish to dedicate this book with affection and gratitude to their parents.

Preface

This book is intended to be a useful, easy-to-read guide to the most common literary references or allusions. What is a literary allusion? How would you know one if you saw one, and what would you do with it?

"It was Greek to me." "He's just tilting at windmills." "Thirty pieces of silver." "The Trojan horse." These are literary allusions.

Brave New World. Oedipus complex. Lot's wife. Rosencrantz and Guildenstern. Tweedledum and Tweedledee. *In Dubious Battle.* These, too, are literary allusions.

Why do we say, "As rich as Croesus"? What does it mean to have an albatross around one's neck? Where did we get the expression "hoist with his own petard"? If someone calls you a Jonah, is he praising or insulting you? If your teacher says to the class, "Don't leave just yet—I may have some pearls to toss," what is he really implying about you? By the time you have finished this book, you will have the answers to these and many other questions.

A literary allusion may be a name, a reference to an incident, a figure of speech, a phrase, or a complete sentence. In any case, it is either a direct or indirect quotation from some literary source. In English, the most common sources of such references are the Bible and Shakespeare, although many other works of literature are referred to by knowledgeable authors.

Allusions are not merely decorative. They are a very convenient and economical way of expressing certain ideas, of focusing the reader's perception of characters, scenes, and events in such a way as to shed light upon the author's purpose. For instance, an author could tell us at some length how sinister a character looks, describing his arched eyebrows, wickedly leering smile, and so forth; or he could simply say that the character was Mephistophelean. Take another example: A writer wants his readers to know that the hero of his story is facing a hopeless task, in which every time he tries to free himself from an entangling situation, the problem only increases in complexity. How convenient it is for him to be able to say that this character's troubles are Hydra-headed, and leave it to the intelligent reader to understand what he is driving at.

This book lists, in alphabetical order, over 1500 of these allusions, or references. Each entry will tell you what the words meant in the original context, and many explain how they might be applied today. You will also find the author and work in which this reference first appeared, wherever it has been possible to do so. An asterisk (*) following a name indicates that additional information about this person may be found in the Appendix on page 281. If there are other entries on the same topic, they are indicated by the words "See also."

A final word about this book: It is not intended as and cannot be a substitute for reading Shakespeare, Homer, Dickens, or the Bible. It merely provides an easy, temporary means of enhancing one's appreciation of what one *is* reading, while at the same time making him aware of what he *should* read when the opportunity presents itself.

1,500
LITERARY
REFERENCES
EVERYONE
SHOULD
KNOW

A

Aaron's rod Moses went with Aaron, his spokesman, to tell Pharaoh to let God's people go. Each time, Pharaoh repeatedly refused, and Aaron would either throw down his rod or gesture with it, and a miracle would occur. After the Exodus, when the Israelites' faith in God faltered, God caused Aaron's rod to sprout buds as a sign that he and his descendants had been chosen as priests.   —Bible, Exod. 7–12; Num. 16–17.   See also: burning bush; Moses; Passover.

Abel —See: Cain.

above suspicion Too reputable to be suspected of doing anything wrong.   —Plutarch,* *Life of Julius Caesar.*

Abraham Descendant of Noah, selected by God to be the father of the nation of Israel. His wife Sarah, who had always been barren, miraculously bore him a son (Isaac) in their old age.   —Bible, Gen. 12, 21.   See also: Isaac; Ishmael.

Abraham's bosom The repose in death of those who have led virtuous lives. Addressing a largely Jewish audience, the writer was speaking of resting, after death, upon the breast of Abraham, the founder of the Hebrew nation.   —Bible, Luke 16:22.

Absalom   Absalom, the beloved but treacherous third son of King David of Israel, took the throne from his father. When he was killed by David's soldiers, David mourned, "O my son Absalom! My son, my son Absalom! Would God I had died for thee . . . !"   —Bible, II Sam. 13—18.   See also: David.

Achilles' heel   The one weak spot in a person who otherwise cannot be harmed. According to Greek legend, Achilles' mother dipped him in the river Styx, when he was a child, in order to make him invulnerable. She held him by one heel when she did so, and this spot was not touched by the magic waters. Later in his life, Achilles was killed when the Trojan Paris shot an arrow into his heel.   See also: Trojan War.

across the river and into the trees   A paraphrase of the dying words of American Confederate General Thomas J. "Stonewall" Jackson: "Let us cross over the river, and rest under the trees." Ernest Hemingway's* novel of this title was published in 1950.

Adam   The first man, created by God from dust on the sixth day. Like Adam, all men return to dust (the earth) when they die.   —Bible, Gen. 2:7.   See also: Eden; Eve; serpent; tree of knowledge; tree of life.

Adam's rib   —See: Eve.

Admirable Crichton   A person gifted with many outstanding abilities or talents. The original was James Crichton (1560–1585), a Scottish traveler, swordsman, and scholar. Used as the title of J. M. Barrie's* play, *The Admiral Crichton* (1902).

Adonis   In classical mythology, a very handsome young man, beloved by Venus.

advise and consent   According to the U.S. Constitution, the President has the power to appoint various federal officers, including members of his cabinet, subject to the "advice and consent of the Senate." Title of Allen Drury's novel (1959) about Washington politics.   —Article II, Sec. 2, par. 2.

after the fall   The fall of man from God's grace—that is, the expulsion of Adam and Eve from the Garden of Eden when they disobeyed God—is described in the third chapter of the Book of Genesis. After the fall, God condemned Adam and Eve to a life of toil and suffering.   See also: serpent; tree of knowledge.

after many a summer dies the swan   Tithonus, who was granted immortality but not eternal youth, grew old and helpless. His existence unbearable, he longed for the release of death, noting enviously that all living things in time "decay and fall," that "after many a summer dies the swan,"—like every other creature—and that "cruel immortality consumed" him alone.
—Alfred, Lord Tennyson,* "Tithonus." See also: swan song.

Ah! Wilderness   This title of Eugene O'Neill's* play, about a young man's coming of age, is a paraphrase of FitzGerald's "Oh, wilderness were paradise enow!" That is, even a barren place would be paradise enough if he could have "A book of verses . . ., a jug of wine, a loaf of bread," and his lover beside him. The passage praises the enjoyment of simple, earthy, romantic pleasures.   —Edward FitzGerald* (translator), *The Ru-báiyát of Omar Khayyám.*

Ahab   King of Israel, he married the wicked Jezebel, who killed the prophets of God and influenced Ahab to worship Baal, a pagan god. Thus, Ahab offended God more than all the kings who preceded him. He was killed in battle under dishonorable circumstances, and "the dogs licked up his blood." Ahab is also the name of the captain of the whaling ship *Pequod* in Herman Melville's* 19th century novel *Moby Dick.*   —Bible, I Kings 16–22; II Chron. 18.   See also: Baal; Jezebel; lord of the flies.

Aladdin's lamp   When Aladdin rubbed his magic lamp, a genie would appear and grant him whatever he wished for. The story of Aladdin is one of many found in *The Arabian Nights' Entertainments,* a collection of ancient Oriental tales.

Alas, poor Yorick!   Prince Hamlet strikes up a conversation with a gravedigger, who comes upon the skull of Yorick, the deceased king's jester, with whom Hamlet romped when he was a child. Taking the skull, Hamlet says, "Alas, poor Yorick! I knew him, Horatio." He then muses on human mortality and the fact that all of our energies, achievements, and concerns come, finally, to this end.   —William Shakespeare, *Hamlet,* act 5, sc. 1.

albatross around one's neck   The poet tells how a sailor thoughtlessly killed an albatross, a symbol of good luck. When the ship was becalmed and the crew were dying of thirst, they hung the dead bird about the sailor's neck to represent his guilt. Thus, if a person has an albatross around his neck, he is burdened with something or someone that reflects discredit on him.   —Samuel Taylor Coleridge,* "The Rime of the Ancient Mariner."

Alexander the Great   King of Macedonia from 356 to 323 B.C., conqueror of the East. According to legend (but not fact), he wept because he had no new worlds to conquer.   See also: Diogenes.

Alice   The main character in *Alice's Adventures in Wonderland* and *Through The Looking-Glass* who dreams bizarre, fantastic adventures. Apparently seven years old, she is a curious, forthright, eager little girl; spirited but proper and amenable, as befits her Victorian upbringing. She seems at once simple and precocious, and is alternately delighted and impatient with the nonsense she encounters.   —Lewis Carroll.*

alien corn   Reflecting on the immortality of the nightingale, the poet speculates that the song he hears it singing was heard by the biblical Ruth as she reaped grain in the foreign land (Judah) where she had gone after her husband's death.   —John Keats,* *"Ode to a Nightingale."*   See also: whither thou goest.

All art is quite useless.   The last sentence in the preface to Oscar Wilde's* novel *The Picture of Dorian Gray* (1891), this statement means precisely what it says. It rounds out the writer's earlier observations that "The artist is the creator of beautiful things" and "The only excuse for making a useless thing is that one admires it intensely."

All the brothers were valiant . . . and all the sisters virtuous.   —inscription on the tomb of the Duchess of Newcastle, Westminster Abbey.

all creatures great and small   As a result of the harrowing ordeal he experiences because of his cruelly indifferent killing of an albatross, a sailor learns that: "He prayeth best, who loveth best/All things both great and small . . ."   That is, unless man loves "Both man and birds and beast," God, who made all these creatures, will not hear his prayers.   —Samuel Taylor Coleridge,* "The Rime of the Ancient Mariner."   See also: albatross around one's neck.

all gods dead, all wars fought   The attitude of the so-called lost generation, who, in fighting or at least living through what seemed the ultimate war (World War I, 1914–1918), found themselves deeply disillusioned and embittered by the experience.

all honorable men   In his cleverly incendiary funeral oration over the corpse of Julius Caesar, Mark Antony professes to believe that the men who assassinated Caesar are honest and selfless. The phrase "honorable men," which he continually repeats to punctuate his remarks on all the good Caesar has done, sounds more and more ironic.   —William Shakespeare, *Julius Caesar*, act 3, sc. 2.

All hope abandon, ye who enter here. The words inscribed over the doorway leading to Hell. —Dante,* *The Inferno* (Part I of *The Divine Comedy*).

. . . all is vanity. For all his work, a man gains nothing that will last. —Bible, Eccles. 1:2. See also: nothing new under the sun; the sun also rises; there is a season.

all the king's men From the nursery rhyme "Humpty Dumpty": Humpty Dumpty had a great fall; / All the king's horses / And all the king's men / Couldn't put Humpty Dumpty in his place again. As the title of the novel (1946) by Robert Penn Warren, this phrase suggests the charisma of the central figure and the supportive efforts of those who surround him.

all my sins remembered Thinking of what he considers his unpardonable lack of resolve in dealing with his father's murderer, Hamlet sees Ophelia, the pure and innocent girl he loves, and says, "Nymph, in thy orisons [prayers], Be all my sins remembered." That is, he asks her to pray for his forgiveness. —William Shakespeare, *Hamlet*, act 3, sc. 1.

all the perfumes of Arabia Tormented by her conscience, Lady Macbeth walks in her sleep, reliving the part she played in the murder of the king. Imagining that blood is still on her hands, she says, "All the perfumes of Arabia" will not remove the sickening smell of it. —William Shakespeare, *Macbeth*, act 5, sc. 1.

all the traffic will bear   The pricing policy of greedy and unprincipled railroad magnates: Charge as much as the traffic on the railroad—the demand for its services enables one to get away with. From American writer Frank Norris' novel *The Octopus* (1901), depicting the struggle for power between the California wheat ranchers and the railroad.

all things to all men   St. Paul the Apostle writes that God has enabled him to be like all of the different people to whom he is obligated to preach the gospel. This makes it possible for him "by all means to save some," for they will be more likely to listen to him.   —Bible, I Cor. 9:22.

all this, and heaven too   A creditably unassuming pastor, who, considering himself more comfortable in this life than he had any right to expect to be, marveled that he also should expect to go to heaven.   —Rev. Philip Henry (1639–1691).

all the world and time   —See: world enough and time.

Alpha and Omega   God's description of Himself in the dream of St. John the Divine. These are the first and last letters of the Greek alphabet; thus God is the beginning and the end of all creation.   —Bible, Rev. 1:11; 22:13.

Alphonse and Gaston   Two excessively polite French gentlemen featured in an early 20th century comic strip by Frederick Burr Opper.

always true to you, in my fashion   —See: gone with the wind.

American dream, the   The idea that a man may have the opportunity to advance himself without restriction, by his own enterprise, and regardless of his background—loosely, to succeed independently. Ideas of what constitutes success run the gamut from the crass to the excellent, and the dream is often blurred or debased. Many consider F. Scott Fitzgerald's* novel *The Great Gatsby* (1925) a classic treatment of the subject, depicting as it does a romantic idealist whose dream leaves "foul dust" behind it.

amor vincit omnia   Latin: "Love conquers all"—but what kind of love, romantic or divine? It depends on the context, of course. Sometimes the motto is ambiguous, as seems to be the case with the nun in Geoffrey Chaucer's* *Canterbury Tales.*

amour propre   Latin: Literally, "love of oneself."

ancient and honorable   The leader(s) of a nation, descended from a long line of fine tradition.   —Bible, Isa. 9:15.

ancient mariner   The central figure in an eerie ballad where an old sailor who buttonholes a total stranger and "holds him with his glittering eye" forces the fellow to listen spellbound to the mariner's strange story of his supernatural experience on the high seas.   —Samuel Taylor Coleridge,* "The Rime of the Ancient Mariner."   See also: albatross around one's neck; all creatures great and small.

another part of the forest   Stage direction used in several of Shakespeare's plays.

ant and the grasshopper, the   In the fable, the ant worked very hard to store up food for the coming winter, while the grasshopper played and sang all day long. When the bad weather arrived, the ant was warm and well-fed, while the grasshopper regretted his earlier behavior, since he now had nothing. —*Aesop's* Fables.

antic disposition   Hamlet tells his friends that, for reasons of his own, he may sometimes pretend to be insane, or put on an antic disposition.   —William Shakespeare, *Hamlet,* act 1, sc. 5.

anvil chorus   In Giuseppe Verdi's opera, *Il Trovatore* (The Troubadour), a chorus sung by a band of gypsies, accompanying themselves upon several anvils.

Apocalypse   A prophetic revelation, in the form of a dream or vision, forecasting the violent end of the world and last judgment of men.   —Bible, the Book of Revelation.   See also: four horsemen of the Apocalypse.

apochryphal   Of doubtful authenticity. The word comes from the Apocrypha, those Old Testament books of the Bible which are not generally included because of their questionable origin.

Apollo   In Greek mythology, the sun god. He is often associated with wisdom, poetry, and music.

Apollyon   The king of hell and angel of the bottomless pit.   —Bible, Rev. 9:11.

apple   —See: serpent.

apple of discord   Some object or issue which causes dispute or argument. The goddess Eris, uninvited to a wedding, appeared at the feast and threw upon the table a golden apple "for the most beautiful." Paris was called upon to judge which goddess merited the title, and his choice of Aphrodite led to the Trojan War.

apple of one's eye   That which one favors or considers most important.   —Bible, Deut. 32:10; Ps. 17:8; Prov. 7:2.

April is the cruelest month   Because it mingles memory and desire, and breeds new life out of the dead remains of the past.   —T. S. Eliot,* "The Waste Land."

Archenemy   Satan; the devil.   —John Milton,* *Paradise Lost.* See also: *Paradise Lost.*

Areopagitica   The Areopagus was the name of a hill (that of Ares, god of war) near the Acropolis in Athens, as well as of a supreme court. John Milton's* *Areopagitica* is a tract, addressed to the English Parliament, advocating freedom of the press. The title implies that Parliament is as august a body as that ancient court, and of similar integrity and prestige. The areopagus was generally believed to be an independent, representative body as much as a court, and its members were elected by the citizens. It is in this tract that Milton observes, ". . . as good almost kill a man as kill [suppress] a good book . . ." He says that whereas a man is a reasonable creature, a book is reason itself.

Ariel   As the name suggests, a light and airy spirit who is able to perform miraculous feats for his master, the enchanter Prospero. He is ultimately freed from that service.   —William Shakespeare, *The Tempest.*

Ark of the Covenant   A rectangular wooden chest overlaid with gold, adorned with golden cherubim and fitted with golden rings through which staves could be passed so that it could be carried. In it reposed the stone tablets on which were inscribed the Ten Commandments, which signified the covenant (agreement) between God and his chosen people.   —Bible, Exod. 37; 40; I Kings 8:9.

Armageddon   A place to which the beast—the evil one—calls on all "the kings of the earth," who worship him, to do battle against the forces of God, led by Christ, at the end of the world.   —Bible, Rev. 16:16.

armies of the night   —See: clash by night.

art for art's sake   To produce objects of fine art—paintings, statuary, music, literature—for the purpose of enjoying them rather than in order to accomplish some moral or social purpose.   —See also: all art is quite useless.

Artful Dodger   A brash but likable London street urchin trained to be an accomplished pickpocket, one of several such boys in the employ of the scoundrel Fagin.   —Charles Dickens,* *Oliver Twist*.   See also: Fagin.

as flies to wanton boys   We men are subject to the cruel whims or impulses of the gods, who toy with us and destroy us as carelessly as boys torment and kill flies.   —William Shakespeare, *King Lear*, act 4, sc. 1.

as idle as a painted ship upon a painted ocean   A seaman's apt description of the utter stillness of his ship, becalmed in mid-ocean.   —Samuel Taylor Coleridge,* "The Rime of the Ancient Mariner."

as sounding brass or a tinkling cymbal   The expression means mere noise, empty of significance and force. St. Paul says that although he may speak very eloquently—"with the tongues of . . . angels"—if he does not have charity, or love, his speech will not signify anything.   —Bible, I Cor. 13:1.

as a thief in the night   —See: children of the night, the.

as though butter would not melt in one's mouth As though one were so mild as to be free of the heat or passions which move most people.   —John Heywood,* *Proverbs.*

ashes to ashes, dust to dust With these words, the body of one deceased is committed to the earth or sea, "in sure and certain hope of the resurrection."   —Book of Common Prayer (the burial service).

ask not what your country can do for you . . . ". . . ask what you can do for your country." An encouragement to sacrifice one's selfish interests to the common cause, in the words of Oliver Wendell Holmes, Jr., of whose statement this is a paraphrase: ". . . to recall what our country has done for . . . us and to ask . . . what we can do . . . in return." —John F. Kennedy, inaugural address.

at heaven's gate As the poet, who has been cursing his fate, thinks of his beloved, his heart rises like the lark that ascends at daybreak and "sings hymns at heaven's gate."   —William Shakespeare, Sonnet 29.

at one fell swoop The image is that of a bird of prey—a falcon, perhaps—which descends with terrible and lethal suddenness to claim its victim. In this instance, the bird is a murderous tyrant and his victims, an innocent woman and her children, are described as "pretty chickens and their dam [mother]." —William Shakespeare, *Macbeth,* act 4, sc. 3.

Avalon   The island across the Western seas where the mortally wounded King Arthur is taken after his defeat by the treacherous Modred. In Avalon, it is understood, he will be received triumphantly and his wounds healed, and there is the intimation that he will one day return to bring Britain to glory.

ave atque vale   Latin: Literally, "hail and farewell"—i.e., I or we respectfully greet you and at once bid you goodbye. —Catullus, *Odes*.

(an ax) to grind   This expression refers to someone (often, though not always, a politician) who curries favor with others in order to achieve his own (hidden) goals.   —Charles Miner, *Essays from the Desk of Poor Robert the Scribe*.

B

Baal   Any of several pagan gods worshipped in Canaan or Palestine. From time to time the Israelites, who entered these regions after fleeing Egypt, turned away from their own God to serve Baal.   See also: Ahab; Jezebel; lord of the flies.

Babbitt   George Babbitt, the central figure in the 1922 novel *Babbitt*, is a businessman who goes along unquestioningly with dull, unoriginal middle-class standards and conventional practices and modes of behavior.   —Sinclair Lewis,* *Babbitt.*

Babylon   Capital city of ancient Babylonia, famous for its hanging gardens. The city has become a symbol of luxury, decadence, corruption, and wickedness and is sometimes personified as a whore.   —Bible, Rev. 17:5.

Babylonian captivity   The period of seventy years when the Jews were enslaved in Babylon, after having been captured by King Nebuchadnezzar.   —Bible, II Kings 24:10–16.

Baconian theory   The theory that Francis Bacon* actually wrote the plays and poems ascribed to Shakespeare. Bacon is only one of several contemporaries of Shakespeare who have been put forward as the "real" author. Most of these theories stem from the belief that the great literature could not have been composed by a man of such little travel experience and formal education as Shakespeare's. Most scholars give little credence to these theories.

Balaam's ass   As Balaam rode on an ass to see the king, an angel appeared to the animal and it turned aside and fell down. Since Balaam could not see the angel, he beat the ass. God "opened the mouth of the ass," and she spoke to Balaam, complaining that since she had always served him well, he should not strike her. Then God "opened the eyes of Balaam, and he saw the angel . . . and he fell flat on his face."   —Bible, Num. 22.

band of angels   In the spiritual "Swing Low, Sweet Chariot," the Negro slave figuratively "looked over Jordan," longing for deliverance from bondage and entrance into heaven, as the people of Judah had looked towards Jerusalem from Babylon, where they had been carried as captives of King Nebuchadnezzar. The Negro envisioned the approach of a chariot which would "carry [him] home." Robert Penn Warren's novel *Band of Angels* was published in 1955.

bar sinister   In heraldry (the design of a knightly crest or coat of arms), a stripe running diagonally from upper right (*dexter* in Latin) to lower left *(sinister)*, rather than the reverse. Commonly (but wrongly) thought to indicate that the bearer of the crest was illegitimate, or at least disreputable.

Barabbas   Shortly before Jesus was crucified, Pontius Pilate went before the mob and offered to turn loose one of the two men then being held for execution. One was Jesus, the other was Barabbas, a convicted murderer. Jesus' enemies in the crowd shouted loudly, "Give us Barabbas," so the criminal was set free and Jesus was crucified.   —Bible, Matt. 27:16–26.

Bard of Avon   A widely used but unofficial title of William Shakespeare. In ancient times bards were gifted composers and/or singers of poetry held in very high regard for their unique gifts. Shakespeare was born in the town of Stratford on (the) Avon (River).

barren ground   In a parable, Jesus told of a farmer who sowed seeds. Some fell on poor ground, and nothing came of them. In the same way, some of the people to whom Christ preached could or would not hear him and would not be saved.   —Bible, Matt. 13:3–9.

baseless fabric of this vision, the   The enchanter Prospero so describes the illusory pageant which he has conjured as an entertainment for his daughter Miranda and her betrothed, Ferdinand. Prospero wistfully observes that "the great globe itself" will eventually dissolve as this vision does and "leave not a rack [trace] behind."   —William Shakespeare, *The Tempest*, act 4, sc. 1.

Bathsheba   Beautiful wife of Uriah, one of King David's soldiers, who became pregnant with David's child. David saw that there was no way to make Uriah believe the child was his (Uriah's), so he wrote a dispatch to his general, telling him to put Uriah into the hottest battle so that he would be killed. Uriah himself carried the dispatch, not knowing what was in it, and he was, in fact, killed.   —Bible, II Sam. 11.

beard the lion in his den   To confront and defy a powerful person in the place where he is most secure; as it were to stride boldly up to the lion and tweak his beard, as portrayed figuratively in Sir Walter Scott's* romantic narrative poem *Marmion,* when Lord Marmion challenges his enemy Douglas in Douglas' powerful castle.

beast with two backs, the   Vulgar image of a man and woman engaged in the sexual act. With this coarse joke,

the speaker (Iago) characterizes that act as animalistic.
—William Shakespeare, *Othello,* act 1, sc. 1.

beat swords into plowshares   After scolding the people of
Judah for their impiety (they offer up sacrifices, but do not
practice charity), the prophet foresees that "in the last days" all
men will abide by the will of God. At that time, God will rebuke
the nations for constantly contending against one another in war,
and they will change their weapons into the tools and implements
of peaceful pursuits.   —Bible, Isa. 2:1–4.

beau geste   Literally, a beautiful gesture—something said or
done with grace and flair which is a token of one's fine instincts.
P.C. Wren's novel of the foreign legion, *Beau Geste* (1924), has
been made into a motion picture several times.

Beauty is in the eye of the beholder.   The quality we
recognize as beauty is not objective, i.e., not inherent in the
object or person described as beautiful. Rather, it is subjective and
determined by the attitude or frame of mind of the one who sees it.
What seems beautiful to one may not seem so to another.
—M. W. Hungerford,* *Molly Bawn* (1878).

beauty is truth   As the poet admires the great beauty of an
ancient Greek urn and contemplates the scenes depicted on its
sides, he is moved to reflect on time and immortality. Noting that
in those scenes time has been arrested, he sees that condition as a
kind of immortality in which anticipation is endlessly prolonged.
The love of man and maid, for example, is "forever warm and still
to be enjoy'd" (our italics), and is thus far superior to "all

breathing human passion." He concludes that the urn, which "tease(s) us out of thought/As doth eternity," is a perpetual reminder to succeeding generations that all we can know on earth, and all we need to know, is that "Beauty is truth, truth beauty."   —John Keats,* "Ode on a Grecian Urn."

because it is there   The reply of a famous alpinist when asked why he wanted to climb Mt. Everest. Simply because it is there, proud, forbidding and inviolate, it beckons and challenges him.   —George Leigh Mallory.

Becky Sharp   The central figure of the novel *Vanity Fair* (1848); an attractive, willful young woman who, as her name implies, is shrewdly and ruthlessly attentive to her own interests.   —William Makepeace Thackeray.*

Beelzebub   —See: lord of the flies.

Before the cock crows, thou shalt deny me thrice. When Peter assures Christ that he will not desert him, no matter how great the danger, Christ replies that Peter will, in fact, deny that he knows him three times before the cock crows. In spite of his good intentions, Peter, fearing for his life because of his association with Christ, does deny him. When the cock crows, he remembers what Christ said, and weeps.   —Bible, Matt. 26:33-34; 69–75.

behemoth   A huge, strong beast. God tells Job that he (God) created this great animal and provides for him and can destroy him. The point seems to be that if such an imposing creature is subject to God's power, surely man is, too.   —Bible, Job 40:15–24. See also: leviathan.

behold a pale horse —See: four horsemen of the Apocalypse.

believe it or not This is the title of a syndicated newspaper feature, begun by Robert L. Ripley in 1918 and still being published, over thirty years after his death. It depicts a great variety of curious or bizarre facts.

bell, book and candle Objects used in the ceremony of excommunication. The phrase may be used either to represent all of the formidable power of the Church to punish those who break its laws; or, derisively, to ridicule the trappings and elaborate rituals of the Church's ceremonies. It is also sometimes used to mean magic or sorcery.   —Sir Thomas Malory,* Le Morte d'Arthur.

bell the cat To do something difficult and dangerous. In a fable, some rats decide that if they can fasten a bell to the cat, they will hear it coming and be able to avoid it. But which of them has enough audacity to do it?   —Aesop,* "The Rats and the Cat."

below the salt In an inferior place. In former times, salt, befitting its importance and value as a commodity or medium of exchange, was kept in a large silver container in the middle of the lord's long table. Persons of distinction sat *above* the salt—i.e., between it and the head of the household; people of lower rank sat at the other half of the table.

Belshazzar's feast   When he dined, the Babylonian King Belshazzar, son of Nebuchadnezzar, used sacred vessels from the captive Israelites' temple. Suddenly a hand appeared and wrote mysterious words upon the wall. The King's wise men could not read them, but Nebuchadnezzar's Israelite protege Daniel said they forecast Belshazzar's ruin, and he was right.   —Bible, Dan. 5.   See also: by the rivers of Babylon; Daniel.

bend sinister   —See: bar sinister.

bent twig   A young person's education will shape or give direction to his adult character: "Just as the twig is bent the tree's inclined."   —Alexander Pope,* *Moral Essays.*

Beowulf   Hero of an 8th century epic poem composed in the Old English (Anglo-Saxon) tongue. The story is set in Scandinavia. The first part depicts the young Beowulf's singlehanded triumph over the fearsome troll Grendel and Grendel's mother. In the second part, with the help of one faithful kinsman (his other retainers desert him), Beowulf slays a terrible dragon but is mortally wounded himself. Beowulf embodies all of the uncompromisingly noble traditions of the poet's heathen Germanic heritage, but they are overlaid with the ideals of Christianity, to which the Anglo-Saxons had been converted. In fact, the hero himself is a very Christ-like figure.

beside oneself   When St. Paul was brought before Agrippa, a viceroy of Rome, he explained how he had been converted to Christianity, and said that he preached that Jesus would rise from the dead. Hearing this, the Roman governor Festus scoffed, "Paul, thou art beside thyself"—i.e., divorced from his reason, a madman. Today, this expression is used merely to describe extreme fear of anger in an exaggerated way, not to mean that one is literally insane.   —Bible, Acts 26:24.

best lack all conviction, the   —See: things fall apart.

best of all possible worlds, the   —See: Candide.

better red than dead   The point of view that although being under communist rule is not desirable, it is preferable to dying in a war with a communist enemy. Other conditions have been seen as alternatives preferable to death: ". . . a living dog is better than a dead lion" (Eccles. 9:4) and "it is better to be a fool than to be dead" (Robert Louis Stevenson,* *Virginibus Puerisque* II). This attitude is considered sensible or cowardly, depending upon the individual. The classic expression of the opposite point of view is Patrick Henry's ". . . give me liberty or give me death."

better to reign in hell than serve in heaven   Satan's defiant statement to his lieutenant, Beelzebub, after God has cast them and all the other rebel angels into hell for warring against the Almighty.   —John Milton,* *Paradise Lost.* See also: *Paradise Lost.*

beyond the pale   Outside of a protected area. A pale is one of a set of stakes or pickets in the fence about an enclosed preserve. If one says or does something that is beyond the pale, he may expect to be criticized.

bid fair   To seem likely. If it bids fair to rain, chances are it will.

Big Brother   —See: *1984.*

bird of dawning   The rooster, which crows to signal the arrival of dawn.   —William Shakespeare, *Hamlet*, act 1, sc. 1.

black hole of Calcutta, the   A room, 18 feet by 14 feet, used as a dungeon by the British East India Company. When the ruler of Bengal rose up against the company in 1756 and its fort surrendered, it was alleged that 146 Englishmen were confined overnight in this stifling room with virtually no ventilation. According to some witnesses, 123 people died as a result. Although not all historians agree on the truth of this incident, the expression "black hole of Calcutta" has continued to stand for an inhuman place of punishment or detention.

Black Prince, the   Eldest son and heir apparent of the English King Edward III; a great warrior who won several important battles in the Hundred Years' War with France. The epithet *Black* may allude to his armor; or it may be attributable to dark hair and complexion, although most members of that dynasty (the Plantagenets) were fair. Ironically the Black Prince died, in bed, before his father did, and never ascended the throne.

blind leading the blind, the   An ignorant or uninformed person trying to instruct or guide another person equally "in the dark" is comparable to one blind man leading another; "both shall fall into the ditch," Jesus said.   —Bible, Matt. 15:14.

blind seer   A prophet who, although unable to see the physical world around him, is, ironically, capable of perceiving the truth of things, present and future, more clearly than those who have their eyesight. Most of us have "blind spots"—i.e., there are things we are not aware of because we are blinded to them (by our pride, for example). Tiresias, in the Oedipus plays of the Greek tragic playwright Sophocles, is a classic example of the blind seer.

blithe spirit   Many poets, inspired by the skylark's sweet song, have addressed it as a creature of exceptional joy which is, as this term conveys, blissfully able to free itself at will from the mundane and mournful cares which earthbound man must endure. The bird is usually associated with morning and the rising sun. English playwright, actor, and composer Noel Coward wrote a play called *Blithe Spirit* (1941).   —Percy Bysshe Shelley,* *To a Skylark.*   See also: divine madness.

blood-dimmed tide, the   A flood of death and destruction which the poet envisions inundating the world as men lose their grasp of any moral direction and their sense of unity and common purpose, and resort to violence and war.   —William Butler Yeats,* "The Second Coming."

Blood is thicker than water.   The common or shared blood that flows in the veins of members of the same family or clan, uniting them against others, especially in a crisis.   —Sir Walter Scott,* *Guy Mannering.*

blood money   Money paid to someone for betraying, or giving evidence against, someone else. When Judas, remorseful over his betrayal of Jesus, flings down the thirty pieces of silver with which he was bribed, the priests do not put it into the temple treasury "because it is the price of blood."   —Bible, Matt. 27:6.

blood of the lamb   —See: washed in the blood of the lamb.

blood, sweat, and tears   In May 1940, Winston Churchill,* in his first statement as Prime Minister of Great Britain, told the British people that all he had to offer them was "blood, toil, tears, and sweat." This was at a time when England was faced with the threat of attack and/or invasion by Hitler's armies.   —John Donne,* *An Anatomy of the World.*

blood will tell   Sooner or later, a person's ancestry—the good or bad blood that he has inherited from his family line—will inevitably cause him to behave in such a way as to achieve eminence, mediocrity, or disgrace.

blot on the escutcheon   Literally, a stain on one's coat of arms. Figuratively, something which hurts one's reputation. —Miguel de Cervantes,* *Don Quixote.*

blow hot and cold   It is not natural for one's breath to blow both hot and cold—i.e., with passion and indifference—at once. Such a person is not to be trusted.   —Aesop,* "The Man and The Satyr."

bone of contention   Whatever people quarrel or argue about, as several dogs might contend—i.e., vie or compete savagely—for possession of a single bone.

bone to pick   "I have a bone to pick with you" means "We have something important and/or unpleasant to settle." The analogy is to two dogs fighting over one bone.

book of hours   A book of the prayers, which a devout and pious person was expected to offer up at certain hours of the day, prescribed by the medieval Church. Such books were richly and elaborately illuminated by monastic scribes, often according to the specifications of the wealthy persons who commissioned them.

born again   Jesus tells the sympathetic Pharisee Nicodemus that if a man is not born again—i.e., "born of water," or baptized "and of the spirit," not the flesh—"he cannot enter into the kingdom of God." Jesus is talking about a spiritual renewal through him.   —Bible, John 3:3.

born with a silver spoon in one's mouth   Someone said to be born in this manner is heir to a life of wealth and ease.   —Miguel de Cervantes,* *Don Quixote.*

Boswell   James Boswell's* biography of Dr. Samuel Johnson,* a distinguished 18th century lexicographer, writer, critic, and raconteur, is generally considered a classic of the form. This is attributable not only to Boswell's readable style, but also to the fact that he made himself Johnson's virtually constant companion, observing him at close range over a period of years, noting his behavior and recording his words at length and in detail. Thus a "Boswell" is one who makes it his business to capture a person's character and personality by means of an extended first-hand study.

bottomless pit   Hell; according to the dream-vision of St. John the Divine, the region from which various agents of torment are loosed to punish Godless men on earth just before the second coming of Christ. Satan is confined there for a thousand years after his defeat by Christ.   —Bible, Rev. 9:1–12; 20:1–3.

brainstorm   *Noun:* a spontaneous, spectacular idea or insight. *Verb:* to coax brainstorms, perhaps unorthodox, perhaps at random, and test them against or in combination with those of others in a group.

brave new world   Miranda, a girl raised on a desert island, is struck with wonder when she first beholds several Europeans of noble and royal rank who have been shipwrecked there. Judging them by their appearance, she concludes that the new world from which they come must be brave (excellent) indeed. In fact, most of these men have practiced deceit, treachery, and debauchery; thus her father, who knows them, observes drily, "'Tis new to thee." English novelist Aldous Huxley's book *Brave New World* was published in 1932.   —William Shakespeare, *The Tempest,* act 5, sc. 1.

bread and circuses The government of Rome pacified the populace with hand-outs of food and bloody, spectacular entertainments in the Colosseum. Thus the people were seduced into a state of irresponsible preoccupation, content to let the government have its way as long as it granted them their pleasures.   —Juvenal,* *Satires.*

bread upon the waters Figuratively, to cast bread upon the waters means to do good deeds, for they will be repaid.   —Bible, Eccles. 11:1.

breaking of nations, the The separation of nations into warring camps.   —Thomas Hardy,* "In Time of 'The Breaking of Nations.'"

bride of Christ The new, or heavenly, city of Jerusalem, seen descending "as a bride adorned for her husband" in the dream-vision of St. John the Divine; by extension, the Church, through which men will reach the heavenly Jerusalem. —Bible, Rev. 19:7–8; 21:2; 22:17.

Brobdingnagian   —See: *Gulliver's Travels.*

Brutus Roman patriot and beloved friend of Julius Caesar. Persuaded that Caesar is becoming a tyrant and endangering the

Republic, Brutus sadly but sternly puts aside his love for Caesar and joins in his assassination. In the play *Julius Caesar*, William Shakespeare dramatizes Brutus' tragic experience.

build a better mousetrap If you "do your thing" better than anyone else, people will come to you no matter where you may be located. The actual words are "If a man . . . make a better mouse-trap . . . the world will make a beaten path to his door."   —Ralph Waldo Emerson* (reportedly used in a lecture; perhaps a paraphrase of the idea as set down in his journal. Elbert Hubbard claimed to have originated this expression.)

buried life, the The poet says that buried and locked up in the heart of every man is his true self, what he really feels, the knowledge of "Whence our lives come and where they go"; but one rarely, if ever, is able to discern it.   —Matthew Arnold, "The Buried Life."   See also: know thyself.

burn the candle at both ends To live a very taxing, fast-paced life, active to or beyond the limit of one's stamina. Of course, the candle will burn out twice as fast at it would if lit only at one end.   —Samuel Hoffenstein, *Songs of Fairly Utter Despair;* Edna St. Vincent Millay, "First Fig."

burn with a hard, gem-like flame "To maintain this ecstasy"—a steady, acute, incandescent enthusiasm—is, says the 19th century English essayist and critic Walter Pater, to succeed in life.   —Walter Pater, *The School of Giorgione.*

burning bright "Tyger! Tyger!"—marveling at the awful aspect of the beast, the poet envisions it "burning bright/In the forests of the night" and speculates about its creator: "Did he who made the Lamb make thee?"   —William Blake,* *Songs of Experience,* "The Tiger."

burning bush When Moses was tending a flock, the angel of God appeared to him in a flaming bush. Then God spoke to Moses from the bush, telling him he would lead the Israelites out of slavery in Egypt.   —Bible, Exod. 3.   See also: Aaron's rod; land flowing with milk and honey; Moses.

burnt offerings Sacrificial animals, ritually burned as an offering to God. There is always the danger that the originally pious purpose of the sacrifice may become subordinate to the ritual itself—that it may be done by rote or for the sake of appearances.   —Bible, Hos. 6:6.

butt-ends of one's days, the The sorry, sordid remains of one's day-to-day existence which have accumulated like the disordered array of stale and crumpled cigarette butts in an ashtray.   —T. S. Eliot,* "The Love Song of J. Alfred Prufrock."

butt of a joke, the The object or victim of a joke; the person at whom it is directed. A butt is anything solid, such as a mound of earth or a tree stump, which provides backing for the target on an archery or firing range.

buz, buz! Thus Prince Hamlet mocks the meddlesome, self-important counselor Polonius, whose prattling he finds so tiresome. It is as if to say, "You don't say so!" or "How the old fool rattles on!" —William Shakespeare, *Hamlet*, act 2, sc.2.

buzz word In a buzz group, a half-dozen or so people carry on a discussion, picking each other's brains and creating a hum of conversation; the subject of their discussion is denoted by the buzz word which has been assigned to that group. Figuratively, a buzz word is a term which has become generally (and perhaps fashionably) evocative, use or recognition of which either signals familiarity with some special area of interest or bespeaks a certain state of mind, and in any case triggers discussion as a stimulus occasions a response.

by hook or crook By one method or another; in any way one can. Originally this expression had a more restricted meaning. In medieval times, manor tenants were permitted to gather firewood by taking whatever underbrush they could cut with a crook, or sickle, and whatever loose timber could be collected from tree limbs with a long-handled hook. —John Wycliffe, *Controversial Tracts*.

by love possessed In the grip of love—as it were, controlled by Aphrodite (or any other deity who is the embodiment of that emotion) in the same way that some are said to be possessed by the devil and therefore unable to behave as their higher instincts might otherwise direct them to. The Greek tragedy *Hippolytus*, by Euripides, is a classic example: Aphrodite causes Phaedra to fall in love with her stepson, and Phaedra, mortified, cannot help herself.   —James Gould Cozzens' novel *By Love Possessed* was published in 1957.

by the pricking of my thumbs One of three witches who are expecting Macbeth to come ask them about the future suddenly feels a prickling sensation in her thumb and recognizes it as a supernatural signal that this evil fellow is about to arrive. She says, "By the pricking of my thumbs,/Something wicked this way comes."   —William Shakespeare, *Macbeth,* act 4, sc. 1.

by the rivers of Babylon The Babylonians under King Nebuchadnezzar captured Jerusalem, destroyed it, and took the Jews into captivity in Babylon. There they "wept when [they] remembered Zion [the fortress district of Jerusalem]." —*Bible,* Ps. 137:1; II Kings 24-25.   See also: Babylon.

cabbages and kings A fragment of the poem, "The Walrus and the Carpenter", recited to Alice by Tweedledee. It is an amusing bit of nonsense in which the walrus benevolently addresses a group of oysters he and the carpenter are about to eat: 'The time has come,' the Walrus said,/'To talk of many things:/ Of shoes—and ships—and sealing-wax—/of cabbages—and kings—'   Thus the line very neatly suggests a very wide range

of topics, from the homely cabbage to a regal monarch.
—Lewis Carroll,* *Through the Looking-Glass.*

Cain   First-born son of Adam and Eve (they literally "raised
Cain"—i.e., brought him up). He was a farmer, whose offering of
crops was rejected by God. His brother Abel, a shepherd, offered
a lamb, which God accepted. Resentful, Cain murdered Abel, and
God drove him away from other men.   —Bible, Gen.
4:1–16. See also: east of Eden; mark of Cain; my brother's
keeper.

cakes and ale   Sir Toby Belch, a coarse reveler, is scolded by
his niece's steward for his roistering. Sir Toby asks the steward if
he thinks that just because *he* is virtuous, everyone else should give
up cakes and ale—i.e., food and drink, the pleasurable things of
life. English novelist and playwright William Somerset Maugham
wrote a novel with this title, published in 1930.   —William
Shakespeare, *Twelfth Night,* act 2, sc. 3.

Caliban   The grotesque and savage offspring of the witch
Sycorax. He is base, treacherous, and surly. He serves his master,
the enchanter Prospero, as a slave. Caliban is motivated by fear
and his appetites, although he shows some signs of being able to
appreciate finer things and, ultimately, to see his faults.
—William Shakespeare, *The Tempest.* See also: Setebos.

Call me Ishmael.   The opening sentence of Herman Melville's* classic tale of whale-hunting, *Moby Dick.* Ishmael, the
narrator, tells how he signed on as a crew member of Captain

Ahab's ship, the *Pequod,* and later participated in many of the major events of the novel.   See also: Ishmael.

call of the wild   Faint echoes of an animal's primitive origins which are buried deep within it and to which it may be aroused, despite ages of domestication, by contact with nature in the wild. Jack London, American novelist, published a book by this name in 1903.

call the tune   To be in charge of the situation; to cause people or events to follow one's direction. An old proverb says that "The man who pays the piper calls the tune."

Calvary   The hill, in or near Jerusalem, where Christ was crucified. The name is from the Latin word meaning "bald," perhaps a reference to the absence of vegetation on the hill's crown, its resemblance to a skull, or the discovery of numerous skulls on the site.   —Bible, Luke 23:33.   See also: Golgotha.

Can (there) any good thing come out of Nazareth? The words of Nathanael upon being told by the Apostle Philip that Jesus of Nazareth was the Messiah. Nathanael (who is sometimes identified with the Apostle Bartholomew) was expressing astonishment that anyone so important could originate in such an inconsequential village; or perhaps disdain for a region (Galilee) which, because it had been overrun so often by invading armies, had a population with a pronounced gentile strain and because of its location, was subject to considerable gentile influence. —Bible, John 1:46.

Can the leopard change his spots? That is, can any creature change the quality which characterizes him, which makes him what he is? The answer to this rhetorical question is no, of course. The prophet says that it is just about as likely that the sinful people of Judah will mend their ways and do good.   —Bible, Jer. 13:23.

Can such things be? Macbeth is appalled when he sees the bloody ghost of a man he has just had murdered. No one else sees the ghost, for it is a figment of his imagination, but he does not realize this. When admonished for raving like a madman, Macbeth replies, "Can such things be" without making us mad?   —William Shakespeare, *Macbeth,* act 3, sc. 4.

Candide A naive and trusting young man who encounters many bizarre and evil characters in his travels. His optimistic old tutor, Dr. Pangloss, nevertheless keeps assuring him that "all is for the best in this best of all possible worlds."   —Voltaire, *Candide* (1759).

Canterbury Tales, The In the Middle Ages, every pious Englishman made a pilgrimage to the shrine of St. Thomas à Becket in Canterbury. *The Canterbury Tales* is a collection of stories bound together by the fiction that they were told by a group of pilgrims—people of all types and classes—on their way to and from Canterbury. This realistic touch, together with a general prologue and interludes of conversational byplay that provide not only a high degree of unity but considerable insight into the storytellers themselves, gives the work a narrative perspective and dimension not unlike that of the novel.
—Geoffrey Chaucer. *

captains and the kings The great men of the world, the imperialists—industrial, military, and governmental leaders —who, says the poet, will pass away in time no matter how powerful and influential they are.   —Rudyard Kipling,* "Recessional."

carrying coals to Newcastle Performing an unnecessary or superfluous job, especially when some service or object is given a person who already has it or has no need of it. An example would be bringing a bouquet to a girl who works in a florist shop. Newcastle, England, was a large coal mining region.

Cassandra A female prophet, usually one who predicts disasters and calamities. In Greek legend she was the daughter of Priam and Hecuba. Her prophecies always came true, but, owing to the workings of Apollo, no one would believe her.   See also: Sibyl.

cast the first stone When a mob was about to throw stones at a woman considered to be a sinner, Jesus suggested that anyone in that crowd who was completely sinless might throw the first stone. Naturally, no stones were thrown.   —Bible, John 8:7.

cast lots To draw straws, etc., so as to decide upon a winner. The Roman soldiers who crucified Jesus cast lots to determine which of them would take possession of his clothing. This event, described in Matthew, was foretold in the Psalms.   —Bible, Ps. 22:18.

cast out the beam out of thine own eye Christ condemns the practice of criticizing minor faults in others ("Let me pull out the mote [speck] out of thine eye") without first correcting our own more serious faults, represented in this metaphor by a beam or timber.   —Bible, Matt. 7:3–5.

castles in Spain This expression can be traced back to a French phrase of the 13th century. It signifies daydreaming, or thinking up wild, impractical schemes. Also "castles in the air."

cat may look on a King There is nothing to prevent one who is humble from merely looking at his superiors.   —John Heywood,* *Proverbs.*

cat on a hot tin roof An image of frenetic activity. If a cat leaps upon a hot tin roof it will scamper wildly about, one way and the other; moreover, its movement will be apparent to anyone under the roof. Used as the title of a play (1955) by Tennessee Williams.*

catch a falling star It is as likely that you will be able to do that, says the poet, as it is that you will be able to find "a woman true, and fair."   —John Donne,* "Song."

catch at a straw   —See: cling to a straw.

catch red-handed To catch someone in the very act of

committing a crime or misdeed, as would be the case if one caught a murderer whose hands were still red with the blood of his victim.

Catch-22   A modern way of phrasing the old adage, "You're damned if you do and damned if you don't." In the novel, set in World War II, the only way soldiers could be relieved of active duty was for them to be mentally incompetent. However, anyone trying to claim he was insane was clearly sane enough to want to get away from the killing and destruction. This was known as a catch-22.   —Joseph Heller.

catharsis   In his analysis of the dramatic form called *tragedy*, Aristotle observed that watching a play of that kind has the desirable effect of cleansing or purging the audience of the emotions of pity and fear, which are evoked by the events depicted on stage—as if the pressure or tension built up in a person by the containment of those emotions were unhealthy. When they are released, one experiences spiritual relief or renewal.   —Aristotle,* *Poetics.*

catspaw   Someone who is being used to do someone else's dirty work. The expression refers to an old fable in which a monkey, wanting to eat some chestnuts which are roasting on a fire, uses the paw of his friend (!) the cat to obtain them.

Cavalier poets   A group of 17th century English court poets united by their loyalty to the King (Charles I) during the civil strife of that period and by the generally dashing, debonair quality of their verse, much of which reflects a disdain for constancy in love.

caveat emptor Latin: "Let the buyer beware." In other words, know what it is you are purchasing before you pay for it.

caverns measureless to man According to the poet's dream-vision, vast underground chambers through which the river Alph runs in the region called Xanadu.   —Samuel Taylor Coleridge,* "Kubla Khan."

cedars of Lebanon   —See: Solomon.

centaur A mythological creature, with the head, arms, and chest of a man and the body and four legs of a horse.

ceremony of innocence The sacred state of innocent virtue, so long revered and the object of worshipful care, which the poet says is drowned in the tide of blood loosed by anarchy and violence in the world—a prelude to the Second Coming of Christ, the end of the world.   —William Butler Yeats,* "The Second Coming."

charge of the Light Brigade The valorous but tragically ill-advised attack by a brigade consisting of 600 lightly armed British cavalrymen against their vastly superior, well entrenched Russian enemy in the Battle of Balaclava (Crimean War, 1854). There was a mixup in orders, and although the troopers could see they did not have a chance against the artillery ranged before them and on both flanks, they charged into "the valley of death," as Tennyson called it, with a magnificent show of courage and

discipline. The brigade was destroyed.   —Alfred, Lord Tennyson,* "The Charge of the Light Brigade."

chariot of fire   The poet imagines himself a warrior fighting to
build Jerusalem "In England's green and pleasant Land"—i.e., to
lodge firmly there the Godly way of life associated with that holy
city. He will lead the struggle riding in this exalted and
inspirational vehicle, which is reminiscent of the passionate
prophet Elijah.   —William Blake,* "Milton." See also:
Elijah.

chariot of the sun   The ancient Greeks thought of the sun as a
fiery chariot driven across the sky by Helios, god of the sun.
Josiah, pious King of Judah, ordered the destruction of the
chariots which had been dedicated to the sun by previous kings
who had turned to the worship of such pagan gods.   —Bible,
II Kings 23:11.

charmed life   Macbeth, told by the witches that he cannot be
harmed by any man born of woman, believes that he leads "a
charmed life." In fact, the witches were merely playing with words:
the man confronting Macbeth at this moment was taken from his
mother in a Caesarean operation and thus, may be said not to
have been born of woman. This man kills Macbeth.   —William
Shakespeare, *Macbeth,* act 5, sc. 8.

Chaunticleer   Central figure in the tale of a vain rooster who
is very proud of his fine crowing. (His name means "clear singer.")
To impress his wife, who derides him for being alarmed by what he
considers a prophetic dream, he throws caution to the wind and is

almost carried off by a fox.   —Geoffrey Chaucer,* *The Canterbury Tales*, "The Nun's Priest's Tale."

Chesterfieldian   Pertaining to the correct manners and dress of proper gentlemen. The name comes from Lord Chesterfield (1694–1773), who wrote a series of letters to his son, advising him on how to conduct himself in various situations.

child is father of the man, the   The poet's image of the unity and continuity of his existence, the shaping of his manhood by his youthful attitudes and experience.   —William Wordsworth,* "My Heart Leaps Up."

children of the night, the   In his First Epistle to the Thessalonians, St. Paul tells them that they are the children of light, not of the night—i.e., they have faith and keep God's Commandments, unlike those "that sleep . . . and . . . are drunken in the night" and will be destroyed when "the day of the Lord so cometh as a thief in the night" to destroy them unaware.   —Bible, I Thess. 5:5.

Chinaman's chance   At the turn of the 20th century, immigrant Chinese settled in large numbers in California and worked for very low wages. Native Californians were greatly opposed to this competition. This situation gave rise to the above saying, with its implication that a Chinese stood very little chance indeed, as far as many Americans were concerned.

Chosen People   This term is frequently applied to the people of Israel, but according to the writer it is "Those who labor in the earth"—i.e., people who work next to the soil—in whom God has deposited "substantial and genuine virtue."   —Thomas Jefferson, *Notes on the State of Virginia.*

circle of compliance   An area within which one can expect his wishes to be complied with. It may be geographical, or it may not be an area at all, but a restricted number of persons wherever they may be.

(nine) circles of Hell   Dante's version of hell, which he called the Inferno (an enormous funnel-shaped pit), was divided into nine regions or circles, each the eternal home of a different type of sinner. For example, the second circle was the hell of carnal and sinful love, the third was intended for the souls of gluttons, and the eighth was for the blasphemers and heretics.   —Dante,* *The Divine Comedy,* Part I: "The Inferno."   See also: first circle.

City of God   The heavenly city of Jerusalem seen in the dream-vision of St. John the Divine. The new Jerusalem comes "down from God out of heaven" after the last judgment, and those who have been saved by Christ enter in. Title of a theological treatise by St. Augustine (A.D. 354–430).   —Bible, Rev. 21.

civil disobedience   A form of protest. Disobedience of civil authority in a civil manner—i.e., a civilized, polite, restrained refusal to obey the laws of the state. The classic model of this behavior was Henry David Thoreau's* denial of his obligation to pay taxes because he was opposed to certain government policies, depicted in his essay (1849) "Civil Disobedience."

clash by night   The poet, troubled by an increasing loss of religious faith (he says it flows away like the ebbing tide), sees himself on a dark battlefield where "ignorant armies clash by night."   —Matthew Arnold, "Dover Beach."

Classical Age   The period during which the civilization and culture of ancient Greece and Rome were ascendant—roughly from the fifth century B.C. to the fifth century A.D.

cling to a straw   To catch hold of anything, no matter how flimsy, in an attempt to support oneself. A drowning man is desperate enough to "cling to a straw" even though he knows his hope of survival is forlorn.   —Bret Harte, "The Luck of Roaring Camp."

Cloud-Cuckoo-Land   A city in the clouds representing an impractical, perfect world.   —Aristophanes, *The Birds*.   See also: Eden; Paradise; Shangri-La; Utopia.

(trailing) clouds of glory   The poet has the sense that we have always existed, that our souls have come "from afar; . . . trailing clouds of glory . . . From God . . ." When we are children, "Heaven lies about us," but eventually "the man perceives it die away."   —William Wordsworth,* "Ode: Intimations of Immortality."

clutch at a straw   —See: cling to a straw.

coast of Bohemia   It has been suggested that Shakespeare's knowledge of continental geography was faulty. For example, the stage direction for act 3, scene 3 of *The Winter's Tale* reads as follows: *Bohemia. A Desert Country near the Sea.* Bohemia, part of what is now Czechoslovakia, is landlocked. However, there have been occasions, prior to Shakespeare's time (for example, from 1269 to 1273), when Bohemia did have access to the Adriatic Sea by virtue of its combination with other nations.

coat of many colors   Jacob (Israel) gave a beautiful coat to his favorite son Joseph. Joseph's eleven older brothers, jealous of him, sold him to the Ishmaelites, who took him to Egypt. The brothers then smeared the coat with goat's blood to convince their father that Joseph had been killed by an animal.   —Bible, Gen. 37:3–36.   See also: Joseph.

Coeur de Lion   The nickname of King Richard I of England—"the lion-hearted."

Cogito ergo sum   A starting point in the search for truth, stated in the Latin of a learned 17th century scholar. It means, "I think, therefore I am [exist]." The philosopher rejects everything he perceives by his senses, but recognizes that in doing this he confirms his own existence (because he thought to do it), as certainly as it is possible to do so. He then sees that the core of his being is thought, which exists apart from the body.   —René Descartes, *A Discourse on Method*.

cold comfort Words which offer little, if any, real comfort.   —William Shakespeare, *King John*, act 5, sc. 7.

collective unconscious Sigmund Freud, the founder of psychoanalysis, said that the unconscious part of a man's mind is a storehouse of information about his past of which he is unaware. According to the psychologist Carl Jung, there is also a *collective* unconscious—a repository of the experiences of the whole human race, evidence of which may be seen in the similarity in theme and symbolism of the folktales of different cultures the world over. For example, the biblical story of the great flood is paralleled in the folklore of other peoples.

comedy of errors A humorous story or play in which the turns of its plot hinge on errors like mistaken identity.

comedy of humors In medieval times it was believed that a man's temperament or humor was determined by the relative amounts of four humors (this word literally means *liquids*) in his body. In a comedy of humors, a single character represents a single humor—e.g., the grump or the optimist.

comedy of manners A humorous play, with witty, sophisticated dialogue which cynically reflects the vices, follies, and idle affectations of the upper classes. The playwright celebrates clever conversation; he does not moralize.

come, fill the cup —with wine. The poet urges his lover to drink and enjoy the sensual pleasures life offers, while there is time.   —Edward FitzGerald* (translator), *The Rubáiyát of Omar Khayyám.*

come home to roost   To return, "like young chickens," to the place of origin and injure the perpetrator or implicate him in what he did.   —Robert Southey, "The Curse of Kehama."

come home with your shield or on it   Uncompromising standing order to the renowned soldiers of the Greek city-state of Sparta: come home victorious or come home dead, borne upon your shield.

come in from the cold   In the "cold war" between communism and the West, no armies meet in the field. Instead, faceless intelligence agents clash in the dark, devious, treacherous grapplings of espionage, unfettered by the ethics, such as they are, of conventional warfare. If an agent can no longer endure such an utterly ruthless and unprincipled kind of existence, he may elect to come in from the cold—i.e., to resign from it. *The Spy Who Came in From the Cold* (1975) is a novel by John Le Carré.

Come now, and let us reason together.   According to the prophet, God, who is angered by the corruption of the Israelites, attempts to reason with them. If they are willing and obedient, he says, they "shall eat the good of the land;" if they are rebellious, they "shall be devoured with the sword."   —Bible, Isa. 1:18.

comic relief   A comic interlude in an otherwise somber or tragic story. Perhaps such a passage is designed to relieve the tension, as the term seems to imply. However, it might be more accurate to say that it provides a leavening, as it were, which makes the action consistent with reality. For life *does* go on, it seems; ironically while some of us suffer, others, preoccupied, enjoy or perhaps merely muddle through.

the company one keeps   One's character is like that of the people with whom he associates, for better or worse. —Euripides, *The Phoenix.*

concentration camp   A stockaded area containing barracks, kitchens, and other like facilities in which persons of a certain class or type are concentrated under guard after being culled from the general population, presumably because they would endanger state security if left at large. At the beginning of World War II, Japanese-Americans were interned for this reason; in Nazi Germany, Jews and people of certain Slavic origin were concentrated in certain areas so that they could be systematically exterminated.

con(fidence) man   A swindler who wins his victims' confidence and trust so that he can separate them from their money or property without the use of force.

conscience of the king   —See: play within a play.

Cordelia   Youngest and most devoted of King Lear's three daughters (her name is from the Latin word for "heart"). A modest, unassuming young woman, her love for Lear never flags

despite his foolishly unjust treatment of her.   —William
Shakespeare, *King Lear*.

corpus delicti Latin: Literally, "the body of the crime"—i.e.,
all of the facts and circumstances of the matter (and not, as many
suppose, merely the corpse of the deceased itself).

courtly love A formal style of passionate, romantic love
practiced by courtiers and the feudal nobility in the late Middle
Ages and celebrated in the literature of the period. The courtly
lover vowed his deep devotion to a lady and became, in effect, her
vassal, putting her on a pedestal and idealizing her even though
she might treat him capriciously. The relationship was adulterous
—there was no possibility of marriage—and romantic because of
its secrecy and the tension caused by the danger of discovery. It
was a curious blending of sensual passion and an idealism which
raised amorousness to a sacred level.

cream of the crop The best of the best; the most excellent of
its kind.

crocodile tears The false, hypocritical tears of affected
sorrow.   —George Chapman, *Eastward Ho* (1605).

Croesus A fabulously wealthy and powerful king of the ancient
land of Lydia. He ruled from 560 to 546 B.C.

crooked shall be made straight, the   Heralding the coming of the Lord, the prophet calls for preparations to receive him: " . . . make straight in the desert a highway for our God." Valleys will be raised up, the mountains leveled," the rough places made plain and the winding path straight.   —Bible, Isa. 40:3–4.

crossing the bar   The poet's euphemistic image of death. He sees himself passing over the sand bar and put out to sea, where he hopes "to see my Pilot [God] face to face."   —Alfred, Lord Tennyson,* "Crossing the Bar."

crossing the Rubicon   When Julius Caesar crossed the Rubicon River in 49 B.C. and entered Rome with his army, he was defying orders and committing an act from which there would be no turning back.   —Plutarch,* *Lives.*

crown of thorns   Shortly before he was crucified, Jesus was subjected to various indignities and tortures, among which was the so-called crown of thorns. This probably consisted of several thorny twigs twisted together into a circle and then pressed down upon Jesus' head. Figuratively, a crown of thorns is any pain or trouble which is thrust upon a person and which he must accept.   —Bible, Matt. 27:29.

crucible   According to the writer, "Faith [is] the one great moving force which we can neither weigh in the balance nor test in the crucible." A crucible is a pot made of a heat-resistant substance in which metal is melted to test it for quality. The word is from the Latin *crucibulum,* a lamp hanging before a crucifix. *The*

Crucible (1953) is a play by Arthur Miller.*   —Harvey
Cushing, *Life of Sir William Osler.*

cruel, only to be kind Hamlet tells his mother that his
seeming cruelty to her is necessary, and that he continues to have
kind feelings for her.   —William Shakespeare, *Hamlet,* act 3,
sc. 4.

cry havoc Havoc, or havock, was an ancient military command to pillage and commit massacre without mercy.
—William Shakespeare, *Julius Caesar,* act 3, sc. 1.

"Curiouser and curiouser!" Alice is repeatedly astonished
by the strange things that happen in Wonderland. On this
occasion she finds herself opening out like a telescope, and "she
was so much surprised, that . . . she quite forgot how to speak
good English."   —Lewis Carroll,* *Alice's Adventures in Wonderland.*

Cyprian, the Aphrodite, the Greek goddess of love, said to
have been born on the island of Cyprus.

Cyrano The dashing, heroic, romantic hero of Edmond Ros-
tand's play, *Cyrano de Bergerac* (1897). Cyrano is a valiant
French soldier who fears no man, but has one disfigurement: a
large nose, about which he is extremely sensitive. He was an
actual person, a French poet living in the 17th century.

D

damn with faint praise To praise in such a weak or restrained manner as to rob the praise of any value. (e.g., "It's not bad"; "Oh, the book's okay, I guess.")   —Alexander Pope,* *Epistle to Dr. Arbuthnot.*

Damon and Pythias Extremely close friends, living in Syracuse in the 4th century B.C. Damon was prepared to give up his life for his friend Pythias, but the tyrannical ruler Dionysius was so affected by this deep friendship that he pardoned them both.

dance of death A sort of morality play which originated in Germany in the 14th century, depicting the character of Death as he leads numbers of men and women, of various classes and conditions, in a dance leading to the grave. At least two dramas with this title have been written, one by August Strindberg in 1901, and one by W. H. Auden in 1933.

dance of the seven veils Salome, a young, beautiful girl, danced before the ruler Herod Antipas, taking off most or all of her clothing as she danced. He was so pleased that he promised to reward her with anything she asked for. Since Salome's mother had been reproved by John the Baptist for living in sin with Herod,

Salome, prompted by her mother, asked for—and was given
—the head of John the Baptist on a platter.   —Bible, Matt.
14:6–11.

Daniel   When the Israelites were his captives, the Babylonian
King selected some of their promising young men to serve him in
the palace. Daniel, called Belteshazzar by the King, was one of
them, and he was bold in maintaining his faith in the God of Israel
despite the King's attempt to indoctrinate him into Babylonian
ways. He also interpreted the King's dreams (because God helped
him), although the King's wise men were unable to do so.
—Bible, Dan. 1–6.   See also: Belshazzar's feast; by the rivers of
Babylon; Daniel in the lions' den; Shadrach, Meshach and
Abednego.

Daniel in the lions' den   When Darius of Persia conquered
Babylon, the Israelite Daniel, who had been a Babylonian captive,
was made a high officer. The princes of Babylon resented having
to report to him and convinced Darius to throw him to the lions for
petitioning the God of Israel instead of Darius, according to law.
Regretfully, Darius did so, but God protected Daniel from the
beasts, and Darius was impressed by God's power.   —Bible,
Dan. 6.   See also: Belshazzar's feast; by the rivers of Babylon;
Daniel; Shadrach, Meshach, and Abednego.

danse macabre   —See: dance of death.

Dark Ages   Broadly, the Middle Ages, the medieval period
—the time between the collapse of the Roman Empire and the
Renaissance (approximately the 5th to the 14th centuries); more

particularly, the 5th to the 10th centuries. These ages were dark in the sense that the light of learning and classical civilization flickered low after the sack of Rome by the barbarians, which shattered the stability of Europe. This was followed by 500 years of chaotic conflict marked by the raids and colonizations of Angles, Saxons, Vikings, and other restless, warlike peoples. The feudal disunity of the next 400 to 500 years was not much more conducive to learning than that darkest period.

Dark Continent   Africa, the home of dark-skinned races. Also, the rest of the world was for a long time "in the dark" regarding this immense continent.

Dark Lady of the Sonnets   The unnamed woman who, some have said, is referred to in a number of William Shakespeare's sonnets. Literary detectives have come up with many solutions to the mystery, but there is no general agreement as to her identity; she may in fact have existed only in the poet's imagination. She is "dark" because she is anonymous, because she has used him cruelly, and because some of the sonnets seem to suggest darkness of hair, eyes, and complexion.

dark Satanic mills   The poet characterizes the factories which had begun to spring up in the Industrial Revolution as a sordid encroachment on natural beauty. He seems to associate these mills' grimy aspect and exploitative practices with the Devil himself, and to see "England's green and pleasant Land" as a link to Christian piety.   —William Blake,* "Milton."

darkness visible   In his description of Hell, the poet uses this paradox to explain how Satan is able to see his dismal domain although God has deprived him of everything that has connotations of goodness, including light.   —John Milton,* *Paradise Lost.*

Darwinian Pertaining to English naturalist Charles Darwin (1809–1882) and his theory of evolution as set forth in his books *The Origin of Species* and *The Descent of Man.* (Actually, Darwin was not the first to suggest evolution, but his books brought the theory to a head with their exhaustive accumulation and scientific evaluation of the evidence.) In pointing to the descent of man from earlier species, evolution has had a profound effect upon religious thought. For example, those who believe literally the Genesis story of creation feel that the theory of evolution is inconsistent with belief in God.

date that will live in infamy, a A date that will be recorded in the annals of disgrace and dishonor. Thus President Franklin D. Roosevelt* characterized Sunday, December 7, 1941, the day on which Japan attacked the U.S. fleet at Pearl Harbor, Hawaii (before war had been declared).   —address to Congress, asking for declaration of war.

David Israel's greatest warrior king. As a boy, he killed the giant Goliath in single combat by using a sling. As King, he conquered Jerusalem by taking its stronghold, Zion; thereafter Jerusalem was the City of David. He is believed to have composed the Book of Psalms. He sinned with Bathsheba, and she later bore his son Solomon, who became famous for his wisdom.   —Bible, II Sam. See also: Bathsheba; Goliath; Solomon.

days of wine and roses This is an image of youth, with its carefree, sensual gaiety, in a poem about the brevity of human life.   —Ernest Dowson,* "Vitae Summa Brevis Spem Nos Vetat Incohare Longam."

De gustibus non disputandum. Latin: "There is no accounting for tastes." Another way of saying "One man's meat is another man's poison."

dead man's hand The poker hand held by Wild Bill Hickock when he was shot in the back: two pairs, aces and eights.

Dean, the The misanthropic satirist Jonathan Swift* was an Anglican clergyman who was appointed Dean of St. Patrick's in 1713.

death, be not proud The poet deflates the awesome and terrible image of Death—" . . . though some have called thee/Mighty and dreadful," he says, " . . . thou art not so." He says that Death is really contemptible; he describes it as merely a "short sleep" before the awakening to eternal life, and ends his sonnet with the neat paradox that Death itself shall die. John Gunther, American author, published a book called *Death Be Not Proud* in 1949.   —John Donne,* *Holy Sonnets.*

death in life The poet's characterization of "the days that are no more"—the past, which is irretrievably lost.   —Alfred, Lord Tennyson,* *The Princess.*

death and taxes   The only two things in this world which are certain.   —Benjamin Franklin,* letter to Jean Baptiste Leroy.

death wish   Some people act in such a way as to suggest that they have an unconscious or perversely instinctive desire to die—they court disaster by saying or doing things that they must know can be fatal. Others acknowledge the wish—e.g., John Keats'* "Now more than ever seems it rich to die . . ." ("Ode to a Nightingale").

Decameron   Written in 1353 by the Italian poet Boccaccio, this book is a collection of one hundred tales. Supposedly these tales were told over a ten-day period by ten people during the 1348 plague in Florence. Decameron in Greek means "ten days."

decline and fall   Edward Gibbon (1737–1794) was the author of the monumental history he called *The Decline and Fall of the Roman Empire*. It is a work notable for its tremendous scope, elegant style, factual accuracy, and diligent if controversial investigation of cause and effect.

deep-damask'd wings   One of the most memorable figures of speech in a poem remarkable for the richness of its imagery. In this passage the color, design, and texture of the tiger-moth's wings are captured in the reference to a lustrous, patterned fabric.   —John Keats,* "The Eve of St. Agnes."

Delilah   A beautiful woman, loved by Samson; the Philistines bribed her to find out how they could capture him. He finally gave in to her persuasion and told her that his great strength came from his long hair (symbolic of his faith in God). She had his head shaved while he slept, and he was taken prisoner. —Bible, Judg. 16. See also: eyeless in Gaza; Philistines; Samson.

deliver us from evil The concluding supplication of the Lord's Prayer, that God lead us away from evil—as he delivered the Israelites from bondage in Egypt.   —Bible, Matt. 6:13.

Delphic oracle In ancient Greece, oracles were gods or their priests or priestesses to whom the people directed questions concerning the future. The most famous oracle was located at the temple of Apollo in Delphi.

deus ex machina Latin: "god from a machine." In many ancient Greek plays there are parts for gods. Since a god presumably would descend from above, the actor playing the role of the god could not simply have walked onto the stage. Instead, he was lowered onto it by means of a mechanical contrivance, the operation of which must have been quite obvious to the audience. Such machines are no longer in use, of course; today the term is used to describe any sudden, artificial and contrived development in the plot of a play or novel which the author resorts to in order to resolve some difficulty.

devil-may-care The attitude expressed by one who says, "The devil may care; I don't." Thus the term means extravagantly reckless and heedless of danger.

devil's advocate   A church official whose duty it is to point out flaws in the evidence of a person's entitlement to sainthood. Since he argues against sainthood, as it were, he is said to be advocating the devil's side. More broadly, a devil's advocate is one who finds whatever legitimate fault he can in someone or something nominated for advancement or distinction.

Dickensian   A term used to refer to the style of writing employed by the English novelist Charles Dickens.* His books are noted for their colorful, quaint characters and their realistic settings, as well as plots which depend a great deal upon coincidence.

die is cast, the   So Julius Caesar is said to have remarked as he crossed the Rubicon River. He was taking a risk, as a gambler does when he throws the dice, and he was prepared to accept whatever outcome chance might dictate.   —Plutarch,* Lives; Suetonius, Lives of the Caesars.

different drummer   A person should have the right to express himself as an individual, even if it means he does not go along with the crowd. Being "out of step" may only mean that he "hears a different drummer."   —Henry David Thoreau,* Walden.

Diogenes   The cynic philosophers believed that virtue was the only end worth pursuing. Diogenes (c. 412–323 B.C.), the foremost of them, dramatized the difficulty of finding an honest man by carrying a lantern, even during the day, as he searched for one. Diogenes exemplified the cynics' high regard for independence when he responded to Alexander the Great's inquiry if there were anything he could do for him. Diogenes coolly replied, "Yes. Stand out of my sunlight."

dirge of the dying year   An image of the west wind, which is associated with autumn, when the year is approaching its wintry death. The poet describes the wind's sound as mournful, like a funeral hymn.   ——Percy Bysshe Shelley,* "Ode to the West Wind."

Discretion is the better part of valor.   Sir John Falstaff's explanation of why he pretended to be dead rather than fight Douglas, the rebel Scot. He meant that acting with caution is safer and therefore preferable to bravery.   ——William Shakespeare, *Henry IV*, Part I, act 5, sc. 4.

distant drum   The poet says one should live for today and not worry about what may come tomorrow. The threat of an unhappy future is compared to the rumble of a distant drum.   ——Edward FitzGerald (translator),* *The Rubáiyát of Omar Khayyám*.

Dives   In Jesus' parable of the rich man and Lazarus, the rich man is sometimes referred to as Dives, although that name does not appear in either the King James or Douay versions of the Bible. The Latin word for "rich," it did appear in the Vulgate edition. ——Bible, Luke 16:19–31.

Divine Comedy, The   An epic poem written in the early 14th century by Dante Alighieri.* It tells of the poet's vision of being conducted by Virgil through Hell and Purgatory and by Beatrice and St. Bernard through several Heavens.

divine madness   To be mad is to be out of touch with the reality which most of us perceive. Does one who is mad apprehend a higher reality? Is his madness actually an ecstatic awareness of divine truth which eludes the rest of us? The Greeks who celebrated the god Bacchus induced a drunken state of "madness." In *To a Sky-lark (1805)*, William Wordsworth* speaks of the bird he exalts as being drunk with divine rapture and having a madness about it; Percy Bysshe Shelley* extols the Skylark in similar terms.

Of course, madness is sometimes attributed to a person who is considered dangerous because he dissents from the "sane" majority view, whereas, according to the poet Emily Dickinson,* his "Madness is divinest Sense."

do and die   The soldier's duty is to follow orders immediately and without question, even if it is obvious that in doing so he will be killed: "Theirs not to make reply,/Theirs not to reason why/Theirs but to do and die."   —Alfred, Lord Tennyson,* *The Charge of the Light Brigade.*

do it with mirrors   To create an illusion, as a stage magician does, by secretly using an arrangement of mirrors to deflect the audience's view from whatever props are required to perform the trick.

do or die   An exhortation to succeed, or die in the attempt.   —John Fletcher, *The Island Princess* (1647); Robert Burns,* "Bannockburn."

Dr. Johnson's dog   Dr. Samuel Johnson* compared a woman preacher to a dog walking on its hind legs: "It is not done well; but you are surprised to find it done at all."   —James Boswell,* *Life of Dr. Johnson.*

dog-day(s)   Usually a reference to a period from early July to early September, marked by the rising of the dog star Sirius, which was formerly supposed to cause the extreme sultriness of that part of the summer and perhaps some of the illnesses associated with it. The term may have another connotation, depending on how it is used.   See also: every dog has its day.

dog in the manger   One who doesn't use what he has, and will not allow others to use it. The phrase comes from the fable of the dog who did not want to eat the hay in his manger, but refused to let the ox eat it.   —Aesop's* *Fables.*

dogs of war   The horrors of war, particularly fire, sword, and famine.   —William Shakespeare, *Julius Caesar,* act 3, sc. 1.

Don't look back.   Because "Something may be gaining on you"—the homespun philosophy of Leroy "Satchel" Paige of baseball fame, a durable pitcher who managed to prevent age from gaining on him a good deal longer than most athletes can. Presumably, he kept looking resolutely ahead.

Dorian Gray   The protagonist in Oscar Wilde's* 1891 novel, *The Picture of Dorian Gray.* Gray remains youthful over the years, living a wild and corrupt life, while his portrait grows old and ugly.

dormouse   A nocturnal rodent. The prefix *dor* is French for "sleep," for the animal is sluggish during the day when it is most likely to be seen. True to his name, the dormouse at the Mad Tea Party that Alice attends in Wonderland is in a very drowsy state and drops off to sleep from time to time during the party.   —Lewis Carroll,* *Alice's Adventures in Wonderland.*

Double, double   Three witches, who are preparing to receive the man whom they know is coming to consult them about the future, mix an evil brew in their caldron and recite charms and spells. They invoke "Double, double, toil and trouble," for it is their purpose to lure this man to his destruction.   —William Shakespeare, *Macbeth,* act 4, sc. 1.

Doubting Thomas   One of Jesus' followers, Thomas, would not believe that his master had risen from the dead until he actually put his hands on the wounds inflicted by Jesus' executioners.   —Bible, John 20:24–29.

down the garden path   —See: primrose path of dalliance.

dragon's teeth   Cadmus, King of Thebes (in ancient Greece) killed a dragon and sowed its teeth like seeds. Armed men immediately sprang up from the places where the "seeds" had fallen and attacked and killed each other.   —Ovid, *Metamorphoses.*

draw a longbow   To exaggerate, stretch out of proportion. The medieval English longbow was a refinement of a very ancient weapon. Noted for its range and accuracy, it was prodigious in size and required a very strong pull.

drawn and quartered, to be　Any of several variations of an exquisitely brutal medieval method of execution, usually reserved for those guilty of treason. Drawing sometimes meant dragging the victim behind a horse; more often it meant evisceration, the extraction of his internal organs. The division of the victim's body into four parts was called quartering, and was accomplished either with an axe or by securing the victim's limbs to four horses and then driving the animals apart. Sometimes a third phase was employed: hanging by the neck so as to strangle the victim almost but not quite to the point of death so that he would have to endure the agony of drawing while still conscious. Quartering, of course, always came last, and finally caused death.

driven off the face of the earth　—See: Cain.

drop in (of) the (a) bucket, a　Thus the prophet describes all the nations of the world and their power, compared to the might of God.　　—Bible, Isa. 40:15.

Dulce et decorum est pro patria mori.　Latin: "It is sweet and becoming to die for one's country."　　—Horace: *III Odes.*

" . . . dust thou art, and unto dust shalt thou return."　—See: Adam.

E

earth moved, the   This phrase may be a reference to a famous image of the sensation produced by sexual consummation: ". . . he felt the earth move out and away from under them." Or, it may be used to sum up, in eloquent simplicity, the startling and profound impact of the theories of Copernicus and Galileo. From time immemorial, men had believed that the earth was the fixed focus of the universe; these revolutionary theories meant that the earth moved——that it had suddenly been reduced to the status of a mere satellite. The phrase may also be an oblique reference to Archimedes' tribute to the lever. He said that if he had a place to stand, he could move the earth.   ——Ernest Hemingway,* *For Whom the Bell Tolls.*

East is East . . .   ". . . and West is West, and never the twain [two] shall meet." Some things are unchangeable, such as the directions of the compass; but, says the poet, "there is neither East nor West . . . when two strong men stand face to face, though they come from the ends of the earth!"   ——Rudyard Kipling,* "The Ballad of East and West."

east of Eden   When Cain was banished by God for killing his brother Abel, he went to "the land of Nod, east of Eden." Earlier, when Cain's parents, Adam and Eve, were driven out of the garden of Eden, God placed angels "at the east of the garden of Eden" to keep them from the tree of life. John Steinbeck* published a novel, *East of Eden,* in 1952.   —Bible, Gen. 3:24; 4:16. See also: Cain; mark of Cain; my brother's keeper.

eat, to drink and to be merry . . ., to   The preacher Ecclesiastes says that it is fitting for a man to enjoy this life that God has given to him.   —Bible, Eccles. 8:15.

eat your cake and have it   It is natural but completely unreasonable to want to "have it both ways"—to have the pleasure of eating your cake without consuming it, so that it is still there to enjoy another day.   —John Heywood,* *Proverbs.*

Ecce homo!   Latin: "Behold the man!" With these words the Roman governor Pilate presented Jesus to the people, who had been incited by the priests to call for his death. (Pilate found no fault in him and hoped the Jews would not insist on his being punished.) When Jesus came out before the crowd, he had been scourged and was wearing the robe and the crown of thorns with which Pilate's soldiers had contemptuously decked him.   —Bible, John 19:5.

Eden   After creating heaven and earth, God created Adam, the first man, and put him into a garden in Eden (commonly believed to be somewhere in the Near East). Here all of Adam's wants were satisfied.   —Bible, Gen. 2:8. See also: Cloud-Cuckoo Land; Paradise; Shangri-La; Utopia.

El Dorado   A fabled land of immense wealth. Originally the name (Spanish for "the gilded") was applied to the King of Manoa, a city on the Amazon River. He supposedly had his entire body covered with oil and then powdered with gold dust. Later the name was applied to his territory, and still later to any fabulously rich region.

elementary, my dear Watson   Apparently these exact words were never uttered by Arthur Conan Doyle's* fictional mastermind Sherlock Holmes, although the comment is made several times in the Holmes films. The expression is meant to give the reader or listener the impression that a particular bit of fine detective work or logical thinking was, for Holmes, very simple.

eleventh hour, at the   At the last possible moment. In a parable, Christ tells the story of men who are hired in the morning to work in a vineyard at a set wage. Other men are hired at various times throughout the day and receive the same wage, even those who are hired one hour before the day's end. The point is, all those who sincerely repent of their sins will enjoy the same blessing, even if they do so at the last moment.   —Bible, Matt. 20:1–16.

Elijah   The prophet who hounded King Ahab of Israel because of Ahab's worship of pagan gods. Ahab's wife, the wicked Jezebel, tried to kill Elijah, but God protected him. After Ahab's death, when Elijah's mission was finished, a chariot of fire drawn by fiery horses appeared and took him up into heaven in a whirlwind.   —Bible, I Kings 17–19; II Kings 2:11.

Elysian Fields   In Greek mythology, Elysium was the home of the blessed. Elysian Fields would be similar to paradise, a land where everyone would be happy.

eminence grise   French: "gray cardinal." In 17th century France, the private secretary of the highly influential Cardinal Richelieu frequently acted, unofficially and confidentially, as the Cardinal's agent, disposing of matters in his name. He was referred to as "gray" because his vestments, like his manner, were unobtrusive, whereas the vestments of a cardinal are bright red. Thus a gray eminence is an inconspicuous third person through whom others must deal with an important figure or organization.

emperor's new clothes, the   In a fable, a vain and foolish emperor was deluded into believing that he was wearing a beautiful new suit of clothes, when in reality he was wearing nothing. It took the innocence of a child in the crowd to cry out that the emperor wasn't wearing any clothes. The others did not have the courage of their convictions, the confidence, and backbone to accept what they saw for what it was—perhaps not simply because they were afraid to flout authority, but because people have a tendency to think that those in charge must know what they're doing, in spite of appearances. —Hans Christian Andersen.*

end of one's tether, the   If an animal is at the end of its tether, it has stretched the rope that restricts its movement as far as it possibly can and may become wild with frustration. A man, too, may be tormented by the realization that he cannot free himself from whatever difficulties beset him. The term is used in the play *The Contrast* (1787) by American author Royall Tyler.

Enoch Arden   The hero of a narrative poem (1864) by Alfred, Lord Tennyson.* He returns home, after having been shipwrecked and stranded on a desert island for seven years, to find that his wife, thinking him dead, has married another. The term is used to describe any long-lost mate returning to find his spouse remarried.

enough rope to hang oneself   If you are opposed to the action someone takes, you might try to leash and restrain him tightly; on the other hand, if you give him enough slack to do as he will, he could very well become entangled in it and destroy himself.   —Proverb.

Epicurean   Epicurus, the Greek philosopher (340–270 B.C.), was the founder of the Epicurean school, which taught that happiness or enjoyment should be life's ultimate goal. The word "epicurean" is often used today in relation to the enjoyment of fine food and drink.

eppure si muove   Italian: "And yet it moves." Galileo had been forced by the Inquisition to deny his belief that the earth revolves around the sun, rather than the opposite. Legend has it that, having thus recanted, he then murmured under his breath, "Eppure si muove." In other words, saying it is so does not make it so.

Esau   First-born (by a matter of moments) of the twin sons of Isaac and Rebekah. Esau was "red, all over like a hairy garment." In adulthood, his brother Jacob extorted the rights to which Esau was entitled as first-born; this showed that Esau despised his birthright, for he should never have surrenderd it no matter how great his hardship. Later, Jacob employed a ruse to get their father to give him the first blessing which should have gone to the elder Esau. Esau hated Jacob for what he had done, but eventually they were reconciled.   —Bible, Gen. 25: 21–34; 27; 33:1–15.

eternal war in man between his reason and his passions A human being is always torn between his higher, God-like intelligence and his baser appetites. He cannot give up either.   —Pascal, *Pensées*. See also; Platonic love.

Et tu, Brute? Latin: "You too, Brutus?" Julius Caesar's dying words to his friend Brutus, who had just stabbed him —William Shakespeare, *Julius Caesar,* act 3, sc. 1.

euphuism From the title character of John Lyly's* *Euphues: The Anatomy of Wit* and *Euphues and His England.* These books are notable primarily for the highly rhetorical and artificially elegant style of expression affected by the author. This style, widely admired and imitated by fashionable Elizabethans, is marked primarily by careful balancing of words, phrases, and clauses.

Eureka! A Greek interjection meaning "I have found [it]!" Archimedes, the inventor, is reported to have exclaimed it upon successful completion of an experiment.

Eve The first woman, created by God from one of Adam's

ribs.   —Bible, Gen. 2:21–25. See also: Adam; Eden; serpent; tree of knowledge.

Every dog has his day. If only once, even the lowliest creature may suddenly and unexpectedly come into his own and find himself in the limelight. Thus Hamlet, with philosophical disdain, addresses the man who has—unreasonably, as Hamlet sees it —provoked him.   —William Shakespeare, *Hamlet*, act 5, sc. 1.   See also: dog-day(s).

Everyman   Central figure in the morality play of the same name (c. 1500), an allegory on the importance of doing good works in this life. "Everyman" is a personification of the whole class of average, universal human beings.

evil that men do lives after them   In his famous funeral oration over Caesar's corpse, Mark Antony observes that if a man has a bad reputation, it will survive him; but "the good [men do] is oft interred with their bones."   —William Shakespeare, *Julius Caesar*, act 3, sc. 2.

Excalibur   The enchanted sword of King Arthur. In one version of the legend he receives it from the mystical Lady of the Lake. Engraved on one side of the blade are the words *Take me,* and on the other, *Cast me away!* After his last battle the grievously wounded Arthur directs his only remaining knight, Bedivere, to hurl it out into the lake. When he does, an arm, "clothed in white samite," emerges to seize it, brandish it three times, and draw it beneath the water.

Excelsior Latin: "more lofty or excellent"; frequently used as a motto (e.g., on a coat of arms).

Exit, pursued by a bear Possibly the most famous stage direction in English. It means just what it says.   —William Shakespeare, *The Winter's Tale*, act 3, sc. 3.

Exodus The title of the second book of the Old Testament, which describes the departure of the Israelites from slavery and oppression in Egypt on their way to the promised land. Leon Uris' novel, *Exodus*, based upon the birth of modern-day Israel, was published in 1958.   See also: Passover; pillar of cloud and fire.

eye of the storm/hurricane Hurricanes and typhoons are whirling circular storms that cover a large area. At the center, or "eye," of the vortex is an area of clear calm, so that as the diameter of the cyclone tracks across a fixed point, a person at that point experiences a brief respite from the savage winds.

eyeless in Gaza When the Philistines captured Samson, they put out his eyes and made him a slave in Gaza. His strength returned as his hair grew, however, and he pulled down the palace of the Philistines, killing them and himself. A novel called *Eyeless in Gaza* was published by Aldous Huxley in 1936   —Bible, Judg. 16:21–31.   See also: Delilah; Philistines; Samson.

eyes have they, but they see not . . . The psalmist condemns idols of silver and gold which are worshipped by the heathen: these idols have unseeing eyes, as well as ears, noses, hands, feet, and throats which do not function, whereas "God hath done whatsoever he hath pleased."   —Bible, Ps. 115:5.

F

face that launched a thousand ships   Paris, Prince of Troy, stole Helen, beautiful wife of the Greek King Menelaus. The Greeks sailed across to Asia Minor to take her back and so began the legendary Trojan War. Helen's beautiful face thus, figuratively, launched the warships.   —Christopher Marlowe, *The Tragical History of Dr. Faustus.*

Faerie Queene, The   An intricately constructed, rhyming epic poem by Edmund Spenser.* Twelve books were projected; six were completed. The poem is an allegory praising moral virtue in general and Queen Elizabeth I in particular. It draws heavily on traditions of chivalry. The Spenserian stanza, devised for this work, was revived two centuries later by several of the Romantic poets.

Fagin   An old man who takes in homeless boys and teaches them to be expert pickpockets and thieves.   —Charles Dickens,* *Oliver Twist.*

fail-safe   Foolproof, safe against failure. The original fail-safe device was meant to prevent the accidental outbreak of a nuclear war.   —Eugene Burdick, *Fail-Safe*.

fair is foul ". . . and foul is fair"—thus three witches establish the principle which informs the action of the play *Macbeth*: an inversion of the natural order of things and the unreliability of appearances.   —William Shakespeare, *Macbeth*, act 1, sc. 1.

fait accompli French: an accomplished fact.

falcon can no longer hear the falconer, the —See: things fall apart.

fall or run on one's sword, to The classic method of suicide for a defeated military commander who prefers death to the disgrace of surrender and sees no alternative. He either persuades a trusted lieutenant to hold the weapon or props it; then he impales himself upon it. It is a gesture which reflects a highly developed sense of honor and the dramatic.

false prophets Men who pretend to be bringers of the truth may instead be vicious and deceitful, even dangerous. —Bible, Matt. 7:15.   See also: wolf in sheep's clothing.

Falstaff A very fat old knight, Sir John Falstaff was friendly with the young Prince Hal, with whom he enjoyed drinking, gambling, and carousing. He thought himself a brave man and a great charmer of the ladies, but he was in fact neither.

—William Shakespeare, *King Henry IV, Parts I and II; King Henry V; The Merry Wives of Windsor.*

familiar spirit   The supernatural attendant of a witch, wizard or sorcerer; it is "familiar" in the sense that it is on intimate terms with its master. It may take the form of an animal—e.g., a cat—and play the role, for all practical purposes, of a sort of mascot. It may also be the spirit of a dead person which is invoked by a medium or spiritualist, as in a seance, in this case, the word "familiar" may also suggest recognition.   —Bible, I Chron. 10:13.

far, far better thing, a   Sydney Carton, who gave up his life so that the woman he loved could marry another man, said the following as he was about to be guillotined: "It is a far, far better thing that I do than I have ever done . . ."   —Charles Dickens,* *A Tale of Two Cities.*

far from the madding crowd   The poet says that humble, country people are insulated from the "madding crowd's ignoble strife"—that is, kept away from the wild scrambling for material gain that most people take part in. Thomas Hardy* wrote a novel, *Far From the Madding Crowd,* published in 1874. —Thomas Gray,* *Elegy Written in a Country Churchyard.*

farewell to arms, a   A withdrawal from combat—the soldier lays down his weapons. Also the title of Ernest Hemingway's* novel (1929) in which the central figure unilaterally resigns from World War I and flees with his lover to neutral Switzerland.

fata morgana   A mirage, illusion, or deception played upon the senses (usually that of sight). There is a mirage with this name which can occasionally be seen near the Straits of Messina in Italy.

fat is in the fire, the   Fat, or grease, falling into an open flame, will cause the fire to flare up. Hence, figuratively the saying means that trouble is being stirred up.   —John Heywood,* *Proverbs.*

fat of the land   The bountiful supply of food issuing from the earth.   —Bible, Gen. 45:18.

fault . . . is not in our stars, but in ourselves, the   Attempting to enlist Brutus in the conspiracy against Caesar, Cassius tells him it is irresponsible to blame astrological influences for the fact that Caesar dominates them: "Men," he says, "at some time are masters of their fates"—i.e., they have themselves and their own inaction to blame.   —William Shakespeare, *Julius Caesar,* act 1, sc. 2.

faun   In Roman mythology, a faun was a being half-goat and half-man, similar to the Greek god Pan. However, while there was only one Pan, there were many fauns, goat-like men with tails, horns, pointed ears, and the legs and feet of goats.

Faust   Dr. Johann Faust, or Faustus, was an astrologer and rascally "magician" who was born in Wurtenberg and died about 1538. Many stories were written in later years using a main character based upon Faust, with Marlowe's and Goethe's* being the best-known examples. In most of these writings, Faust, a seeker after the true meaning of life, sold his soul to the Devil in exchange for youth or knowledge. In the 20th century, this theme was used in Stephen Vincent Benét's story "The Devil and Daniel Webster" and in D. Wallop's *The Year the Yankees Lost the Pennant*, which became the hit musical *Damn Yankees*.

fearful symmetry   The awesomely terrible, if also beautifully designed form (of a predatory beast).   —William Blake,* "The Tiger."

feet of clay   The weakness or imperfection in a seemingly ideal or blameless person. Daniel was called upon by King Nebuchadnezzar to interpret a dream the king had had. In this dream appeared a "great image" or idol which had a head of gold, breast and arms of silver, belly and thighs of brass, legs of iron, and feet of iron mixed with clay.   —Bible, Dan. 2:33.

fiddle while Rome burns   To do something inane or unimportant while earthshaking events unfold all around one. Nero, mad Emperor of Rome, is said to have fiddled while the city was in conflagration. Whatever he did at that time, he could not, of course, have played a fiddle, for there was no such instrument at that time.

fiery furnace   —See: Shadrach, Meshach and Abednego.

Fifth Column, The   A World War II term signifying a systematic organization of spies and saboteurs designed to

fig   78

penetrate the enemy country. The purpose was to obtain information, cause and spread confusion and division among the enemy populace, and assist or join the invading army. The term came into existence when, during the Spanish Civil War (1936–1939), General Moa stated that he had four columns of soldiers advancing on Madrid, plus a fifth column made up of sympathizers within the city which would assist the invaders by attacking from the rear. Ernest Hemingway's* drama *The Fifth Column* was written in 1938.

fig   A common fruit—therefore a mere nothing. If one does not care even a fig, he does not care at all.   —John Heywood,* "Be Merry Friends."

fig leaves   When Adam and Eve, formerly innocent, ate the forbidden fruit, they became aware of good and evil, conscious of shame. Thus they saw their own nakedness, which had meant nothing to them before, and "sewed fig leaves together, and made themselves aprons" to cover it.   —Bible, Gen. 3:7.

filthy lucre   St. Paul stipulates that a man who desires the office of a bishop or that of a deacon must set a good example. Among other things, he should not be greedy for lucre—i.e., worldly riches—which Paul says will defile the man by distracting him from things of the spirit.   —Bible, I Tim. 3:3, 8.

final solution   Hitler's final solution to "the Jewish problem" was systematically to kill them all. Over six million Jews were wiped out, most of them in gas chambers, before World War II came to an end.

fine madness, a   The quality "Which rightly should possess a poet's brain." Poets are generally viewed as somewhat mad, in the sense that they have a perception of things which differs from that of most of us (as is the case with a madman)—a keener, finer, perhaps inspired apprehension of reality.   —Michael Drayton, "To Henry Reynolds, Of Poets and Poesy."

fine and private place, a   Thus the poet ironically describes the grave, adding, "But none, I think, do there embrace." —Andrew Marvell,* "To His Coy Mistress."

fire and brimstone   In the dream or vision of St. John the divine, the wicked are promised torment with fire and brimstone (sulfur), which is the basis for the concept of hell as a place of fiery punishment.   —Bible, Rev. 14:10.

fire and ice   In that part of his *Divine Comedy* called *Inferno*, Dante* takes the reader on a tour of Hell. There, sinners are confined in different regions (circles) and tormented in different ways, depending on the kinds of sins they have committed—some burn, and some freeze. In Robert Frost's* poem "Fire and Ice," he speaks of these two extremes in terms of human desire and hate, respectively. Sometimes this expression is used to characterize a person who is subject to sudden extremes of passion and cold hatred; or capable of either extreme at will and without warning; or in some strange way a combination of both at once.

fire next time, the   After the great Flood, God set a rainbow in the sky as a token of his promise never again to inundate the earth. As an old Negro spiritual points out, however, he never said he would not use fire the next time he becomes fed up with man's wickedness. Also title of novel (1963) by black American writer James Baldwin.

first circle, the   The first (least severe) of the nine regions of Hell depicted in the *Inferno* of Dante's* *Divine Comedy*. Alexander Solzhenitzyn's *The First Circle* describes what we might call the minimum security level of the Soviet penal system under Stalin —certainly not pleasant, but a good deal less harrowing than the hard-labor camps of maximum security.   See also: (nine) circles of Hell; GULAG.

First Folio   The first collection of Shakespeare's thirty-six plays in one volume, published in 1623, edited by Heminges and Condell, members of Shakespeare's acting company, the Lord Chamberlain's Men. About 1,000 copies were printed. Because of the sources used, the method of printing, and careless proofreading, the book is of questionable authority.

first fruits   The earliest of a farmer's crops, suitable for offering to the deity because of their priority and the sacrifice the farmer makes in postponing the satisfaction of his own hunger.   —Bible, Exod. 23:16.

first shall be last, the   The lowliest, most insignificant person will, in the life hereafter, be raised up in importance, while the proud and mighty will be brought down.   —Bible, Matt. 19:30.

fishers of men   Jesus, urging Peter and other fishermen to leave their nets and follow him, told them that he would make them "fishers of men," meaning that they would soon be gathering men around them as they preached and would catch, i.e., save, them from sin and damnation.   —Bible, Matt. 4:19.

flash in the pan   The hammer of a flintlock musket carries a flint. When released, the hammer strikes this flint against a piece of steel above the pan, or open receptacle, of gun-powder, and the resultant spark ignites the powder. If the powder is defective or improperly loaded, it may "flash in the pan," making a spectacular display without discharging the ball.

flower born to blush unseen, a   The poet remarks that many flowers are never seen because they grow in out-of-the-way places, "And waste [their] sweetness on the desert air." By the same token, many men of noble character never achieve recognition because of their humble obscurity.   —Thomas Gray,* "Elegy Written in a Country Churchyard."

fly in the ointment, a   A small detail which spoils everything.   —Bible, Eccles. 10:1.

fool and his money are soon parted, a   A foolish person can easily be swindled out of his money. Also, he will readily spend his money on worthless or foolish things.

foolish consistency is the hobgoblin of little minds . . ., a   Although consistency is often considered a virtue, stubbornly sticking to one point of view without following the dictates of reason is a sign that one is not very intelligent.   —Ralph Waldo Emerson,* "Self-Reliance."

foolish virgins, the   —See: wise and foolish virgins, the.

fools rush in   —where angels fear to tread. The poet means that angels, who have less to fear than mere mortals, are discreet and wise enough to know their own limitations, but fools are not.   —Alexander Pope,* "Essay on Criticism."

forbidden fruit   —See: serpent.

for love or money   Most men are motivated by the expectation of one of these rewards, or both. If one refuses to do something for love or money, he certainly will never do it.

for want of a nail   A seemingly small, insignificant thing can sometimes alter events. "For want of a nail the shoe was lost; for want of a shoe the horse was lost . . ." and so on, until the battle itself was lost.   —Benjamin Franklin,* *Poor Richard's Almanac.*

for whom the bell tolls   Most of us, hearing a funeral bell, might naturally "send to know for whom the bell tolls"—i.e., ask who has died. We should not, however, for "No man is an island"; *any* man's death diminishes each of us, for we are all "involved in mankind." Therefore the bell "tolls for thee." Also the title of

Ernest Hemingway's* novel (1940) in which the central figure discovers that all men are interdependent.   —John Donne,* *Devotions upon Emergent Occasions.*

four horsemen of the Apocalypse, the   Symbolic figures of war, famine, pestilence (plague), and death, all on horseback, seen in the dream or vision of St. John the Divine. The figure of Death is mounted on a "pale" horse.   —Bible, Rev. 6:2–8.   See also: Apocalypse.

Frankenstein   This name does not refer to a monster in the original book, but rather to the monster's creator, a medical student (*not* a doctor). In figurative language, a Frankenstein monster is any idea, object, etc. created by someone which then becomes a threat to its creator.   —Mary Shelley, *Franken-stein.*

Freudian slip   Sigmund Freud, the founder of modern psychology, stated that slips of the tongue are actually a way for the unconscious mind to express itself. For example, a man saying, "Mary, unfortunately my wife, is sick today," may be misplacing the word "unfortunately" because in fact he feels it is unfortunate that Mary is his wife. This is a Freudian slip.

from the horse's mouth   Direct from the source.

from the sublime to the ridiculous   The original meaning of this saying was that there is just a slight difference between that which is sublime, or high in excellence, and that which is foolish.   —Thomas Paine, *Age of Reason*.

funeral oration   A speech to commemorate someone's passing. Mark Antony's is a classic example of eloquent rabble-rousing in which Antony shrewdly plays upon the emotions of a mob by means of irony and subtle indirection. At the beginning Antony pays tribute to the men who assassinated Caesar, men whom the crowd supports; then, gradually and cleverly, he manipulates his audience into a state of raging hostility against the assassins.   —William Shakespeare, *Julius Caesar*, act 3, sc. 2.

Furies   In ancient Greece, it was believed that there were three avenging spirits whose job it was to punish sinners who, for some reason, had eluded justice here on earth. They were called Erinyes or Eumenides.

G

Gadarene swine   Jesus cast devils out of two men and into a herd of swine. Possessed, the animals rushed headlong into the sea and were destroyed.   —Bible, Matt. 8:28–32.

Galahad   In Arthurian legends, one of the purest of the knights of the Round Table, he was the son of Lancelot and Elaine. In some versions of the Arthurian tales it is he who finally discovers the Holy Grail; in other versions it is Gawain; in still others it is Percival.

Galilean, the   An epithet for Jesus, who, although born in Bethlehem in Judea, was raised in Nazareth in Galilee.

Garden   —See: Eden.

Gargantua   In medieval legend, a giant known for his huge appetite. Anything immense or gigantic may be called Gargantuan. The character was adopted by Rabelais for his satire *Gargantua and Pantagruel.*

gather ye rosebuds while ye may   Roses are traditional symbols of sensuality. Here the poet urges maidens to indulge their passions while they have the chance, for "Old Time is still a-flying." The same idea is expressed in very similar terms in Edmund Spenser's* *The Faerie Queene* (II,12) and *The Wisdom of Solomon* (I, 10).   —Robert Herrick,* "To the Virgins to Make Much of Time."

Gawain   Nephew of King Arthur, one of the knights of the Round Table. In some versions of the Arthurian tales, it is Gawain who finds the Holy Grail, in other versions it is Percival; in still others it is Galahad.

generation of vipers   Thus John the Baptist caustically addressed the Pharisees and Sadducees who came to observe him when he was baptizing people in the Jordan River in the wilderness. John was heralding the coming of the Messiah and urging repentance; he saw these groups as poisonous snakes because they were exclusive and complacent in the strict observance of their conservative doctrines. Jesus used the same expression in addressing scribes and Pharisees. (The Scribes were laymen who worked with the Pharisees and thus were part of the priestly establishment which opposed the sweeping changes which Jesus preached.) American author Philip Wylie wrote *A Generation of Vipers* in 1944.   —Bible, Matt. 3:7.

gentleman's agreement   An agreement between two parties based upon mutual trust.

gesture without motion   A paradox, virtually impossible to imagine literally, which nonetheless graphically conveys the futile pretense and impotence of modern man.   —T. S. Eliot,* "The Hollow Men."

Get thee behind me, Satan   Thus Jesus rebuked the apostle Peter, for Peter's earnest and loving wish that Jesus should be spared the suffering he foresaw showed that Peter was less concerned about "the things that be of God" than "those that be of men." Thus Peter's solicitude about Jesus' life in the flesh was comparable to the temptations of Satan, which should be put behind one, out of sight.   —Bible, Matt. 16:23.

get thee to a nunnery   Bitterly disillusioned by the discovery of his uncle's treachery and his mother's infidelity, and disgusted with his own irresoluteness, Prince Hamlet tells Ophelia, the girl he loves, that she should enter a convent rather than marry and become "a breeder of sinners."   —William Shakespeare, *Hamlet,* act 3, sc. 1.

Gilbertian   W. S. Gilbert* (1836–1911), an English satirist, dramatist, poet, librettist, and wit, wrote many works in which his favorite themes were displayed: magic potions and elixirs, foolish old women in love with younger men, identity mixups, etc. However, the quality in his pieces which most deserves the title Gilbertian is that of the topsy-turvy world in which black is (or seems to be) white, day becomes night, the truth seems to be a lie, and vice versa.

gilded age, the   This expression, referring to the U.S. in the last quarter of the 19th century, is a sarcastic echo of the name the Golden Age. "Gilded" means that the object in question is not pure gold, merely gold-plated.   —Mark Twain* and Charles Dudley Warner, *The Gilded Age.*

gird the loins   To bind the region about the hips with clothing or armor before setting out to accomplish something. The expression is usually accompanied by the phrase ". . . like a man."   —Bible, Job 38:3.

give the devil his due   To acknowledge, perhaps grudgingly, whatever positive feature(s) an otherwise hateful person may have. The expression could be applied in a very literal way to John Milton's* portrayal of Satan in *Paradise Lost:* he is as evil as can be, but it is difficult not to be impressed by his colossal pride and steadfast determination.   —Miguel de Cervantes,* *Don Quixote*.

give it back to the Indians   In a fanciful story, "Dan'l" Webster, the great lawyer and U.S. Senator from New Hampshire, debates the devil himself, known as Scratch. Webster is defending a neighbor who has mortgaged his soul to the devil and wants to break the contract. As he accepts the case, Webster observes that ". . . if two New Hampshiremen aren't a match for the devil, we might as well give the country back to the Indians." Thus this phrase denotes disgust with something of no value which was not worth striving for.   —Stephen Vincent Benét,* "The Devil and Daniel Webster."

Give me your tired . . .   ". . . your poor,/Your huddled masses yearning to breathe free,/The wretched refuse of your teeming shore,/Send these, the homeless, tempest-tossed, to me:/I lift my lamp beside the golden door."   —Emma Lazarus, "The New Colossus: Inscription for the Statue of Liberty."

give up the ghost   As Jesus died on the cross, "He gave up the ghost." The word translated as "ghost" can also mean "spirit." Thus giving up the ghost is releasing one's spirit, or whatever we call that part of us that keeps us alive.   —Bible, Luke 23:46.

give us this day . . .   . . . our daily bread. Fourth sentence of the prayer which Jesus stipulates for the faithful, admonishing them not to use "vain repetitions, as the heathen do." This, the Lord's Prayer, is a model of humility and simplicity, for, as Jesus says, "your Father knoweth what things ye have need of, before ye ask him."   —Bible, Matt. 6:11.

glass houses   "Those who live in glass houses should not throw stones" goes the old proverb. In other words, one should be extremely careful of what he says or does to others if he himself is open to attack.   —Geoffrey Chaucer,* *Troilus and Cressida.*

gloria mundi   —See: *sic transit gloria mundi.*

go off half-cocked   The hammer of a flintlock musket must be fully drawn back if it is to fire properly. If it is discharged when at half-cock—i.e., after only one click on the ratchet—the projectile will not have maximum velocity and force.

goat song   The word "tragedy" is derived from the Greek *tragoidia,* meaning "goat song." No one knows for certain why the Greeks called plays of that type by this name; it may be because the dramatic festival was celebrated in connection with the fertility rites of Dionysus, since goats traditionally are associated with lechery.

goatish disposition   Goats have a reputation for stubborn belligerence, but they also connote lechery.

goddams, the   Name given to the English by the French, referring to one of their pet oaths. This term can be traced back at least to the 15th century, and it is known that Joan of Arc used the word often to refer to her English enemies.

God's little acre   Longfellow tells us that the old Anglo-Saxons used to refer to a burial-ground as God's-Acre.
—Henry Wadsworth Longfellow,* "God's Acre."

Gog and Magog   All those great leaders of the earth who are enemies of the Christian church are referred to as Gog and Magog.   —Bible, Rev. 20:8.

gold, and frankincense, and myrrh   These were among the gifts presented to the infant Jesus by the Magi, the wise men from the East. Frankincense is a resin from Arabian trees which is burned to make a fragrant odor; myrrh is also an aromatic resin from the East.   —Bible, Matt. 2:11.

Golden Age, the   This refers to the period in a society's history when it was at its peak of power and glory. For example, England's Golden Age is thought to have been during the reign of Queen Elizabeth I (1558–1603).   —See also: gilded age, the.

golden apples   Fruit of the trees that grew in the legendary garden of Hesperides at the western extremity of the world known to the ancient Greeks. According to an ancient Greek legend, the beautiful Atalanta, a swift runner, declared that she would not marry a man who could not outrun her. She repeatedly defeated her suitors until one dropped three golden apples at intervals in the race. Because she stooped to retrieve them, he was able to win the race.

golden bowl, the   The poet asks if love can be put "in a golden bowl," implying that anything so excellent cannot be contained, no matter how fine the vessel. In Ecclesiastes, the preacher refers to the end of life as the breaking of the golden bowl. —William Blake,* "The Book of Thel"; Bible, Eccles. 12:6.

golden calf While Moses was on Mount Sinai receiving the Ten Commandments from God, the Israelites, not knowing what had become of him, made and worshipped a golden idol in the form of a calf. When Moses saw this, he angrily smashed the tablets on which God had written the Commandments. —Bible, Exod. 32. See also: Ark of the Covenant; Ten Commandments.

golden touch, the Midas was a legendary king who wished that everything he touched would turn to gold. His wish was granted, but when he realized the implications of it—flowers, food, drink, and even his own child became lifeless metal—he regretted it.

Golgotha ". . . a place of a skull." The hill, in or near Jerusalem, where Christ was crucified. The site is identified by this name in three of the Gospels (Matthew, Mark, and John) and as Calvary in the Gospel of St. John. —Bible, Matt. 27:33. See also: Calvary.

Goliath A gigantic soldier, champion of the Philistine army, who challenged the Israelites under Saul to choose a champion to face him. The boy David, Saul's armor bearer, volunteered and felled Goliath with one stone from his sling. David later became king. —Bible, I Sam. 16–17. See also: David; Philistines.

gone with the wind Haunted by passion for his lost love, the poet says he has forgotten much in his attempt to put her out of his mind—it is "gone with the wind," like the roses he has flung in his mad pursuit of oblivion in wine, dance, song, and other women —but she haunts him still. Therefore he can say, somewhat ambiguously, "I have been faithful to thee, Cynara! in my fashion." In Margaret Mitchell's novel of this title, a whole way of life—that of the antebellum Southern planter—is swept away by the tempest of the Civil War.   —Ernest Dowson,* *"Non Sum Qualis Eram Bonae Sub Regno Cynarae."*

good fight, the   St. Paul urges the early Christians to "fight the good fight of faith"—to be righteous, godly, loving, patient, and meek; to be content with little and not seek corrupting wealth. Thus the good fight is a struggle in which one arms oneself only with faith, humility, and a good and strong will.   —Bible, I Tim. 6:12.

good night, sweet prince   Horatio, Hamlet's best friend, bids farewell to the dying Prince in these words. A biography of the great 20th century Shakespearean actor John Barrymore, titled *Good Night, Sweet Prince,* was written in 1944 by Gene Fowler.   —William Shakespeare, *Hamlet,* act 5, sc. 2.

good Samaritan   Jesus tells of a foreigner, in trouble, who was ignored by respectable and ostensibly pious Jews. Surprisingly, he was assisted by a man from Samaria, a place whose inhabitants were generally despised in Judah for their pagan affiliations. The point is that a good neighbor is one who practices charity, or love, even though he may be alien or regarded with aversion.   —Bible, Luke 10:30–36.

good shepherd, the   Jesus preaches that he takes care of his followers as a shepherd should care for his flock, being ready to lay down his life for them.   —Bible, John 10:11.

Gordian knot   In ancient times, a man named Gordius fastened a rope in such a way that it seemed impossible to untie it. Alexander the Great heard that whoever undid the knot would reign over the whole East. He took out his sword and cut the knot with one stroke. Therefore, cutting the Gordian knot means solving a very difficult problem in one brilliant move. —Plutarch,* *Lives.*

go tell the Spartans . . .   ". . . thou who passest by,/That here, obedient to their laws, we lie." An epitaph commemorating the death in battle of a detachment of Spartan soldiers who, dedicated to their city-state's expectations of its army, would not surrender, and died fighting.   —Simonides.

go west, young man   —if you would seek your fortune. This was the advice of Horace Greeley, in a *New York Tribune* editorial, to young men who had no prospects; however, the phrase was not coined by Greeley.   —John Babsone Lane Soule, "Terre Haute Express."

Gorgon   —See: Medusa.

gospel   From the Anglo-Saxon *god,* meaning "good" and *spell* meaning "tale"; specifically, the good news about salvation through Christ, which is told in the first four books of the New Testament. More broadly, the word means that which is undeniably true. A highly popular musical about Jesus Christ, written in 1970 by Stephen Schwartz, is called *Godspell*.

Gotham   New York City. Originally it was the name of an imaginary place in the poem which begins "Three wise men of Gotham/Went to sea in a bowl."

grain of mustard seed, a   In a parable, Jesus compares the kingdom of heaven to a grain of mustard seed. Although it is an extremely small seed, it grows into the greatest of herbs. Later he compares a mustard seed to faith, saying that if a man has only so much faith he can move a mountain.   —Bible, Matt. 13:31—32; 17:20.

grapes of wrath, the   In his dream or vision of the end of the world, St. John the Divine hears an angel announce that the wicked shall drink wine pressed from the grapes of God's anger. These grapes have been growing throughout the period of man's sinful history and are ripe for harvest on the Day of Judgment. Also the title of John Steinbeck's novel (1939) depicting the privation and suffering of American farmworkers during the Depression of the 1930s.   —Bible, Rev. 14:10; 14—20.

grasp at a straw   —See: cling to a straw.

gray eminence   —See: *eminence grise*.

great I am, the   When God speaks to Moses out of a burning bush and calls upon him to lead the Israelites out of bondage in Egypt, Moses asks how he is to refer to God when he speaks to the Israelites. God replies, "I am that I am; . . . say unto [them], I am hath sent me unto you."   —Bible, Exod. 3:14.

great leveler, the   Death is the great leveler, for in death no man is greater than another regardless of the wealth, power, or prestige one may have enjoyed in life.

great unwashed, the   This phrase refers insultingly to the large number of poor, dirty people in a society. No one knows who first used the expression, although it can be traced all the way back to the Greek playwright Aristophanes, who referred in *The Clouds* to "the life of the unwashed."

Great War, the   World War I (1914–1918).

great white hope   When Jack Johnson, a black man, was heavyweight boxing champion (1908–1915), many white men, resenting his preeminence, hoped for the emergence of a white boxer who would be great enough to defeat him.

greater love hath no man . . .   ". . . than this, that a man lay down his life for his friends." Anticipating his death, Jesus tells the apostles to love one another as he has loved them, and refers to the sacrifice he is soon to make for their sake and the sake of all men.   —Bible, John 15:13.

Greek to me   Casca, a "sour" Roman who was to participate in the plot against Julius Caesar, reported that the great orator Cicero* spoke to the people in Greek. He cynically observed that everyone seemed duly impressed, but that it was unintelligible to him.   —William Shakespeare, *Julius Caesar,* act 1, sc. 2.

Greeks bearing gifts   One's enemy should not be trusted, even if he seems to be bringing a gift. The Greek gift of a wooden horse to Troy was full of enemy soldiers; once the horse was pulled within the gates of Troy, the Greek warriors emerged and killed the Trojans.   —Virgil,* *Aeneid.*

green-eyed monster   Jealousy.
—William Shakespeare, *Othello,* act 3, sc. 3.

green pastures   Lush, verdant, comfortable surroundings. "The Lord," says the psalmist, "is my shepherd;" and like a good shepherd, he leads his charges into green pastures and cares for them tenderly. American dramatist Marc Connelly wrote a play, *The Green Pastures,* first produced in 1930.   —Bible, Ps. 23:2.

Grendel   In an Anglo-Saxon epic poem of the 8th century, a terrible ogre which comes out of the misty swamps to terrorize the Danes in their mead-hall, carrying off warriors by the armful to devour them in his den.

grim reaper, the   Death, who impassively harvests the souls of men as a farmer mows down stalks of wheat with his scythe.   —Henry Wadsworth Longfellow,* "The Reaper and the Flower."

grin like a Cheshire cat   In Wonderland, Alice meets a cat which is always grinning complacently. It grins, she is told, "because it's a Cheshire cat." (No one is sure what this allusion means.) The cat also has a way of disappearing and reappearing in different places. On one occasion it disappears gradually, beginning at the tail, and the grin remains some time after the rest of it has gone.   —Lewis Carroll,* *Alice's Adventures in Wonderland.*

groves of academe   The academy, the institution devoted to learning, is compared to a quiet, forested preserve which is conducive to study and the pursuit of truth.   —Horace, *Epistles.*

guilt by association   Assumption that one is involved in unacceptable behavior merely because he has associated with the person who committed it.

Guinevere   King Arthur's beautiful queen, she became the mistress of Sir Lancelot, the greatest of Arthur's knights, and, penitent, entered a convent.

GULAG   An acronym for the Russian words "Chief Administration of Collective Labor Camps," the penal system of Russia during the reign of Joseph Stalin. The Gulag "archipelago" depicted in the book by Alexander Solzhenitzyn is not literally a group of islands. He describes the various installations of the penal system as "islands" in a hidden network that is roughly congruent with the whole expanse of Russia.

Gulliver's Travels   A satirical book which purported to be the actual adventures of one Lemuel Gulliver, shipwrecked in Lilliput, whose inhabitants are one-twelfth his size. On succeeding voyages he visits Brobdingnag, whose inhabitants are gigantic; Laputa, a flying island; and the country of the Houyhnyms, horses of great intelligence who are served by repulsive, ignorant, man-like creatures called Yahoos.   —Jonathan Swift.*

Hades   In Greek mythology, the underworld residence of the dead; equivalent, as far as location is concerned, to the Hebrew Old Testament *Sheol* and the King James Bible's *hell* or *pit*, although in Greek mythology there is no suggestion of the fire and brimstone torment of the biblical hell.

hail and farewell   —See: *ave atque vale.*

hair of the dog   Taking a small amount of alcohol the morning after a night of heavy drinking was thought to be a cure for a hangover. Some people swear by this "hair of the dog that bit you" cure.   —John Heywood,* *Proverbs*.

halt and the blind, the   In a parable, Jesus tells of a man who gave a great banquet and invited many people, all of whom made excuses. Angry, the man sent his servant to "bring in . . . the poor and the maimed, and the halt [those who limp], and the blind"—i.e., the disadvantaged rabble from the streets. Thus God will turn from those he has favored if they ignore his summons to a righteous life in favor of worldly pursuits.   —Bible, Luke 14:21.

handful of dust   An image of death, echoing the biblical "Dust thou art, and unto dust thou shalt return."   —T. S. Eliot,* *The Waste Land*.

hand-in-glove   To say that two people are hand-in-glove means that they are just that close together, that they conform to one another as precisely as a glove fits the hand.   —Jonathan Swift,* *Polite Conversation*.

handwriting on the wall   —See: Belshazzar's feast.

hanging gardens   —See: Babylon.

happy days are here again   Motion picture song adopted by the Democratic party for the presidential campaign of 1932, won by Franklin D. Roosevelt.* The song promises restoration of prosperity after the stock market crash of 1929 and the

Depression which followed, attributed by the Democrats to Republican mismanagement under Herbert Hoover.   —Jack Yellen and Milton Ager.

happy warrior, the   Franklin D. Roosevelt's* characterization of Alfred E. Smith in a nominating speech at the Democratic National Convention of 1924.   —William Wordsworth,* "Character of the Happy Warrior."

harmony not understood   —See: (all) nature is but art unknown to thee.

hat in hand   If you appear before someone with your hat in your hand, you humbly acknowledge your inferiority.

head brought in upon a platter   —See: dance of the seven veils.

heard melodies are sweet   But, says the poet, "those unheard are sweeter still." Addressing the piper depicted on the side of an ancient vase, he urges him to play "to the spirit ditties of no tone." The imagination, he suggests, can produce more exquisite melodies than the ear perceives.   —John Keats,* "Ode on a Grecian Urn."

Heart of Darkness   A novel by Joseph Conrad,* published in 1902, describing a man's journey into the interior of Africa, devoid of the light of civilization. Here he discovers that even the most enlightened and civilized person retains, deep within him, the roots of man's dark and savage ancestry.

heart of the matter, the   This usually means the core or basic fact of a situation, stripped of all embellishments—in the words of Job (19:28), "the root of the matter." Since the heart is traditionally associated with emotion, particularly love, it may also denote the extent to which love is a factor in the situation described. Graham Greene's novel *The Heart of the Matter* was published in 1948.

heart . . . too soon made glad, a   A proud duke who is negotiating a marriage contract says that one of the things that amazed him about his former wife was that she was too easily pleased by "whate'er she looked on"—a sunset, a bough of cherries—and not as impressed with his gifts to her as she ought to have been. (He gave her "a nine-hundred-years-old-name.") —Robert Browning,* "My Last Duchess."

Heathcliff   Central figure in the English novel *Wuthering Heights* (1848), a dark, brooding, tempestuous man capable of towering passions. Rejected by Catherine, the girl he loves, he is bent on revenge and destroys her and himself in pursuing it. —Emily Bronte.

heavenly Jerusalem, the   The holy city of Jerusalem, the City of God made new. In his dream-vision, St. John the Divine sees it coming down from God out of heaven.   —Bible, Rev. 21:2.

heavy-winged thieves Bees, whose wings are laden with the nectar and pollen they take from flowers.   —Percy Bysshe Shelley,* "To a Skylark."

Hell hath no fury like a woman scorned. If a woman turns down a suitor, he may take it philosophically or he may be hurt or angry; but if a man turns down a woman he is risking a retribution that would put hell itself to shame.   —William Congreve,* *The Mourning Bride.*

hell or high water Extreme adversity of any kind, from fire to flood.

Heloise and Abelard In medieval times, the philosopher Pierre Abelard fell in love with a beautiful girl he had been tutoring, Heloise, the niece of the Canon of Notre Dame Cathedral. Their affair ended tragically, with Abelard becoming a monk and Heloise becoming a nun, although they continued to write passionate letters to each other.

here a little, and there a little In small increments, one little portion at a time. Thus, according to the prophet, will God teach his lessons to his people.   —Bible, Isa. 28:10.

Hesperides   —See: golden apples.

hew to the line To chop a tree or trim a log accurately, determinedly close to the guiding line; figuratively, to bear down

on any task with energy, concentration, and purpose.
—Roscoe Conkling, speech nominating President Grant for a third term.   See also: let the chips fall where they may.

hewers of wood and drawers of water   Slaves; those who perform menial tasks like cutting wood and carrying water. The Gibeonites, afraid that the invading Israelites would kill them all, tricked Joshua into a treaty, and the Israelites decided to spare them and use them as laborers.   —Bible, Josh. 9:21.

high crimes and misdemeanors   Among the offenses considered by the U.S. Senate to give sufficient reason for removal from office, on impeachment, of the President, Vice President, or other civil officer.   —U.S. Constitution, Article II, Sec. 4.

Hobson's choice   ". . .—take that or none." A choice which is forced upon one and thus is no choice at all. In *The Spectator,* no. 509, Sir Richard Steele tells of a man named Hobson who had horses for hire and insisted that each customer take the one nearest the door.   —Thomas Ward, *England's Reformation.*

Hogarthian   William Hogarth was an English painter and engraver famous for his realistic and satirical portrayal of 18th century life.

hoi polloi   Greek: "the many"; signifying the common people, the masses. Often preceded erroneously by the word "the."

hoist with his own petard Hamlet says it is fitting that one who sets an explosive device (petard) to injure someone else should be blown up (hoisted) by the thing himself. —William Shakespeare, *Hamlet,* act 3, sc. 4.

hold a mirror up to nature According to Prince Hamlet, this is "the purpose of playing"—i.e., playacting. An actor, he says, should not overdo nature but reflect it and seem natural. —William Shakespeare, *Hamlet,* act 3, sc. 2.

holier than thou Self-satisfied and confident of the superiority of one's own piety to that of everyone else. —Bible, Isa. 65:5.

Holy Ghost The third person of the mystery of the Christian Holy Trinity, with the Father and the Son; God is conceived of as existing in all three persons, and yet not totally in any of them. The Holy Ghost, or Holy Spirit, is God-with-man.

Holy Grail The cup used by Jesus at the Last Supper. In medieval times this legendary cup was the object of knightly quests. Figuratively, any idealistic purpose is a grail. See also: Galahad; Gawain; Percival.

holy of holies The oracle or innermost chamber of the Jewish Temple; the most sacred part of the building, where the Ark of the Covenant was concealed behind a veil or curtain. —Bible, Exod. 40:3; I Kings 8:6.

home from the hill   Part of the epitaph of one who has been brought to his place of origin for burial "under the wide and starry sky":   Home is the sailor, home from the sea,/And the hunter home from the hill   —Robert Louis Stevenson,* *Underwoods,* "Requiem."

honest dullard, an   A characterization of King George III. The writer says that the American Revolution would not have occurred if the King had not been such a man.   —Sir James George Frazer, *The Golden Bough.*

Honi soit qui mal y pense.   Latin: "Shame to him who thinks evil of it"; motto of the oldest British order of Knighthood, the Order of the Garter. Said to have been the remark of King Edward III when he restored to Joan, the "Fair Maid of Kent," the garter she had lost while dancing with him.

honor among thieves   It is ironic—surprising and, perhaps, sardonically amusing—to discover that those who steal and do other dishonorable things often observe a code of honor among themselves, for example by refusing to betray one another.

hook, line, and sinker   If a fish is really fooled by the lure, he may swallow it and these pieces of tackle as well; in some cases, people may be taken in just as completely. Of course, from the point of view of the fisherman, this term may be used to describe a total loss.

hook-nosed fellow of Rome   Julius Caesar, as described by Sir John Falstaff. (Caesar had a prominent, aquiline nose.) Falstaff has just accepted the willing surrender of a knight who was part of the army opposing the King. Now he bombastically tells his general, Prince John, how he (Falstaff) has captured the fellow, managing to suggest that it was quite an exploit by comparing himself to Caesar, who observed, after one of his conquests, that he "came, saw and overcame" *(Veni, vidi, vici).*   —William Shakespeare, *Henry IV,* Part II, act 4, sc. 3.

and hope to have it after all   In the argument (introductory summary) of his book of verse, the poet says he will "sing" of the many simple, earthy pleasures of the country folk, but that he will "sing of Heaven," too, "and hope to have it after all"—i.e., he dares hope that heaven will not hold against him his fondness for those sensual but fundamentally innocent pleasures. —Robert Herrick,* *The Hesperides.*

Horatio Alger   Horatio Alger, Jr. (1832–1899) wrote many popular books on the theme of poor but honest boys growing up to be successful through enterprise and hard work. The term "Horatio Alger story" signifies a rags-to-riches theme, although, strictly speaking, none of the boys in the original Alger books ever become millionaires.

Horatius at the bridge   Heroic Roman defender of the Sublician Bridge over the Tiber River. He and two others volunteered to hold off the enemy on the far shore while the bridge was destroyed behind them. He sent his companions back just before the span collapsed and held the enemy alone; after it fell, he plunged into the river. One account says he survived and was accorded many honors; another says he was wounded by arrows and drowned.

horned moon, the   A crescent moon, which may be said to resemble a bovine animal's horns.   —Samuel Taylor Coleridge,* "The Rime of the Ancient Mariner."

horns of a dilemma   A dilemma is a set of equally undesirable alternatives: the horns may be those of an animal, like a bull, or the cusps of a crescent moon. In either case, the image suggests the severe discomfort one would experience in knowing that he would have to suffer the sharp pricking of one tine or the other, or, if he seizes them, of being tossed this way or that. —Laurence Sterne, *Tristram Shandy.*

(The) horror! The horror!   The dying words of Mr. Kurtz, a charismatic ivory trader who penetrates the Dark Continent of Africa. Isolated deep in the interior, he experiences "the awakening of . . . brutal instincts . . . and . . . monstrous passions." Dying, he cries out at some awful image of his experience that returns to him at that moment.   —Joseph Conrad,* *Heart of Darkness.*

horse of a different color   In Shakespeare's *Twelfth Night* (act 2, sc. 3), Sir Toby Belch correctly guesses Maria's intention, and she nods, "My purpose is, indeed, a horse of that color." If it were not, it would require explanation and reconsideration.

Hotspur   Henry Percy (1364–1403), eldest son of the first Earl of Northumberland. His nickname reflects his personality—impulsive, bold, ardent; always impatient to spur his horse forward in the charge like the medieval knight he epitomizes. Chivalric honor is his prime motivation.   —William Shakespeare, *Richard II; Henry IV*, Part I.

house divided, a   Lincoln referred to the biblical quotation in comparing our nation to a house. Neither one can stand for long if it is split in two.   —Bible, Mark 3:25.

How are the mighty fallen!   Thus David laments the death of the great Israelite king Saul and his son Jonathan, killed in a battle with the Philistines.   —Bible, II Sam. 1:25.

How many angels can dance on the head of a pin?   A subject of idle and protracted debate. Certain medieval philosophers and theologians are said to have speculated and argued at great length on this problem. The answer, of course, is unknowable, and it is difficult to see why it would matter anyway.

How many divisions has the Pope?   This sarcastic inquiry by Joseph Stalin reflects the disdain of that pragmatic atheist, whose massive Red Army was made up of hundreds of divisions, for the chief of the tiny Papal State. When he heard it, Pope Pius XII said, "Tell my son Joseph he will meet my divisions in heaven."

how sharper than a serpent's tooth   Thus King Lear describes how it feels "to have a thankless child." He is wounded by his daughters' ingratitude.   —William Shakespeare, *King Lear,* act 1, sc. 4.

human comedy   A comedy is a drama with a happy ending or one which deals with serious matters in a light or comic way. Dante's* *The Divine Comedy* explores hell and heaven, deals with God and the devil, and has cosmic scope; human comedies confine themselves to this world and an examination of the abundant variey of types found in the human species and of their interesting interactions. Both Honoré de Balzac* and William Saroyan wrote books called *The Human Comedy*.

Humanism   Throughout the Dark Ages, the Church and its dogma dominated European society; faith in God and expectation of the hereafter occupied most of the attention of most men, and the human experience as such was scorned. With the emergence of classical learning in the Renaissance (ironically, it had been harbored by the Church), men began to take new interest in themselves as men, and in secular things like art, for they saw this interest reflected in the classics.

Hydra-headed   One of the twelve labors of Hercules, in Greek legend, was to kill the many-headed monster, the Hydra. Whenever Hercules cut off one of the creature's heads, two more heads immediately appeared in its place. A Hydra-headed problem is one which only increases in difficulty as one combats it.

Hyperion   According to Greek myth, a Titan who is the father of Helios, the sun god; thus one who is bright; magnificent and heroic.

I

I am become Death, the shatterer of worlds. Quoted by Dr. J. Robert Oppenheimer, architect of the atomic bomb, upon the successful test of that device in 1945. The words come from the *Bhagavad-Gita*, a very early Hindu poem.

I am a part of all that I have met.   The aged Ulysses (Odysseus), dissatisfied with his dull and idle existence, reflects proudly on the experiences of his active youth—the Trojan War and his ten years' wandering afterwards. He has, he says, left his stamp indelibly upon all the places and persons with whom he has come in contact, and they on him. He resolves "to sail beyond the sunset . . .; To strive, to seek, to find and not to yield."   —Alfred, Lord Tennyson,* *Ulysses.*

I am the law.   So said Frank Hague, long-time mayor of Jersey City (1917–1947), and it was no idle boast—certainly not within the precincts of that municipality, at any rate.

I am the state.   A characteristically egotistical and imperious statement attributed to Louis XIV, King of France (1643–1715), who styled himself the Sun King. In French: *L'etat c'est moi.*

I came, I saw, I conquered.   The inscription carried before
the procession marking one of Julius Caesar's triumphs—in Latin:
Veni, vidi, vici.   —Suetonius, *Lives of the Caesars.*

I could not care less.   This means "It is impossible for me to
care any less than I do." Frequently misstated as "I could care
less," which seems to imply at least a modicum of concern, thus
robbing the remark of its force. Of course it could be put in the
form of a rhetorical question: "Could I care less?"

I know nothing except the fact of my ignorance.   A
principal tenet of Socratic thought, which, if rigorously adhered
to, will enable one to approach the truth; for if a mere man is
satisfied that he knows a good deal, is convinced that he is not in
error, his mind will be rigid and closed.

I only am escaped alone to tell thee.   So Job is told by a
succession of messengers who come to report the disasters which
have befallen him—the loss of his livestock, his servants, and his
sons. This is used as the title of the epilogue of Herman Melville's*
novel *Moby Dick,* as Ishmael, the narrator, is the sole survivor of
the whaling ship *Pequod.*   —Bible, Job 1:13–19.

I wash my hands of it.   Pilate, Roman Procurator of Judea,
was reluctant to condemn Jesus. Pilate found no fault with him,
and, besides, Pilate's wife had had a premonitory dream and told
her husband to have "nothing to do with that just man." When
Pilate told the Jews he wanted to release Jesus, however, they
would not relent, and he saw that it would be politically
inexpedient to override their wishes; so he symbolically "washed

his hands before the multitude, saying, 'I am innocent of the blood of this just person.'" —Bible, Matt. 27:24. See also: INRI.

I'm from Missouri. Missouri is the "Show Me State." One who is—or says he is—from Missouri does not believe anything until he sees it. —Willard Duncan Vandiver, speech.

Iago The supreme villain, evil from top to toe. Angry because he has not been promoted, and suspecting that Othello has had an affair with his wife, Iago malevolently slanders Othello's innocent wife, Desdemona. Convinced that she has been unfaithful, Othello murders her. —William Shakespeare, *Othello*.

Icarus and Daedalus In Greek mythology Daedalus and his son Icarus made wings for themselves which they attached by means of wax. They were thus able to fly, but Icarus flew too close to the sun, which melted the wax, and he fell into the sea.

Ides of March A fatal date, the 15th day of March, which Julius Caesar was warned by a soothsayer to beware. Caesar was in fact assassinated on that day in 44 B.C. American dramatist and novelist Thornton Wilder published a novel called *The Ides of March* in 1948. —William Shakespeare, *Julius Caesar*, act 1, sc. 2; act 3, sc. 1, Plutarch,* *Lives*.

idols with feet of clay —See: feet of clay.

If music be the food of love . . . ". . . play on," Orsino,

Duke of Illyria, tells his musicians. Seized by the melancholy conventionally attributed to one in love, he wishes that his appetite (his love) may be glutted "and so die."   —William Shake-speare, *Twelfth Night,* act 1, sc. 1.

in a brown study   Not a room, but a state of mind—lost in thought, abstracted, rapt. It is brown, perhaps, because the dull neutrality of that color suggests the apparent suspension of the individual's faculties.   —John Lyly,* *Euphues.*

in cold blood   Without any passionate impulse. It is at least natural and human to strike out in anger. One who commits violence coolly seems essentially inhuman, and "neither can nor should be forgiven." Truman Capote's account of a senseless mass-murder, *In Cold Blood,* was published in 1965. —George Bernard Shaw*, *Man and Superman.*

in dubious battle   Languishing in Hell soon after his fall from Heaven, Satan speaks to his lieutenant Beelzebub of the war they fought against God "on the Plains of Heav'n." He professes to believe that the outcome was, at the time they fought, uncertain. John Steinbeck's* novel *In Dubious Battle* appeared in 1936.   —John Milton,* *Paradise Lost.*

In hoc signo vinces   Latin: "In this sign shalt thou conquer." The Roman Emperor Constantine claimed to have had a vision, before his battle with Maxentius, in which these words were emblazoned in the sky together with an image of the Cross. When he did in fact win the battle, Constantine converted to Chris-tianity.   —Eusebius, *Life of Constantine.*

INRI The initial letters of the Latin *Iesus Nazarenus Rex Iudaeorum:* "Jesus of Nazareth, King of the Jews." This legend was affixed to the Cross above the head of the suffering Jesus. It mockingly denoted his crime—his allegedly having claimed to be a king without Roman authorization. In fact, as Jesus said, his kingdom was "not of this world," but the high priests trumped up the charge; when Pilate asked him if he claimed that title, Jesus, knowing he must suffer, replied merely, "Thou sayest it." Thus Pilate could not risk having it reported to Rome that he had countenanced a man's setting himself up as king.   —Bible, Matt. 27:35–36.

In the beginning . . . The opening phrase of the Book of Genesis, in the Bible, which tells of the creation of the universe and of the creatures which inhabit it. The Book of John also begins with the same three words.

In the midst of life . . . . . . we are in death. That is, all mortals are constantly in danger of death and continually move toward it.   —Book of Common Prayer (the burial service).

in the same breath When one makes a remark and then immediately—as it were, not even pausing to breathe—follows it with another, usually more or less contradictory; the latter is said to have been spoken in the same breath.

in sorrow thou shalt bring forth children One of the multiplicity of sorrows God promises Eve in punishment for her disobedience.   —Bible, Gen. 3:16.

in the twinkling of an eye   In the microfragment of an instant it takes for the eye to reflect a flash of light, the corruptible body will be transmuted into a spiritual substance when the dead are resurrected.   —Bible, I Cor. 15:52.

In (by) this sign shalt thou conquer   —See: *In hoc signo vinces.*

infant crying in the night . . ., an   The poet, contemplating the untimely death of his friend, says that he can only trust that all such apparently senseless and wasteful losses will somehow contribute to the ultimate good. This, he says, is his dream; but he *knows* no more than does an inarticulate infant which is afraid of the dark.   —Alfred, Lord Tennyson,* *In Memoriam.*

inherit the wind   Probably a variation of *reap the whirlwind. Inherit the Wind* is the name of a play by Jerome Lawrence and Robert E. Lee (first produced in 1955), depicting the Scopes "Monkey Trial" of 1925.   See also: sow the wind.

instruments of darkness   The Scottish general Banquo warns his "noble partner" Macbeth that witches are the tools, or agents, of evil and try to win our confidence only to betray us in the end. Macbeth seems quite impressed, nonetheless, by the fact that a witch's prophecy about him has just been fulfilled. —William Shakespeare, *Macbeth,* act 1, sc. 3.

into that good night   Into death. Although the poet characterizes it as good—suggesting rest and peace after travail;

perhaps that death is, after all, fitting—he also says a man is obligated not to yield his life passively.   —Dylan Thomas,* "Do Not Go Gentle into that Good Night."   See also: rage, rage against the dying of the light.

into your tent I'll creep   The titillating promise made by a dashing Bedouin chieftain to the woman he loves, who waits longingly for him to come and carry her away into the desert—although she may make a token show of protest and struggle. The romantic reputation of the sheik was established and enhanced by many films popular in the 1920's, especially those starring Rudolph Valentino. This line comes from the 1921 song "The Sheik of Araby" by Harry B. Smith, Frances Wheeler, and Ted Snyder.

inward ripeness   Spiritual, intellectual, emotional maturity, as opposed to chronological or physical adulthood.   —John Milton,* "On His Having Arrived at the Age of Twenty-three."

iron hand in a velvet glove   This expression may be interpreted to mean that one should treat others with care and respect, meanwhile remaining firm inwardly. The 19th century British historian Thomas Carlyle attributed this expression to King Charles V of France.

Is there no balm in Gilead?   Gilead was a region noted for its balm, a soothing medicinal substance; it would be astonishing not to find any there. The prophet is expressing his incredulity and anguish over the fact that there seems to be no source of spiritual healing in Jerusalem, the very footstool of God. Jerusalem's spiritual physicians do not minister to the people; they are corrupted by idolatry.   —Bible, Jer. 8:22.

Isaac Beloved son of Abraham and Sarah. God tested Abraham's faith by telling him to kill Isaac as an offering to God. As Abraham prepared to do so, God stopped him, and Abraham looked up and saw a ram caught in a thicket. He used the ram for his sacrifice. This may be seen as an example of the way God provides for those who are faithful.   —Bible, Gen. 22. See also: Providence.

Isaiah The greatest of the prophets; the Book of Isaiah actually contains the words not only of Isaiah himself but of two later anonymous prophets. Isaiah's work is notable for his advocacy of God's universality and holiness and for what some later writers have interpreted as a prophecy of the birth of the Messiah: ". . . a virgin shall conceive and bear a son, and shall call his name Immanuel."   —Bible, Isa. 7:10–16.

Ishmael Natural son of Abraham and his wife's handmaid, Hagar. God said he would be a wild man, that he would be opposed to all men and they to him, and that he would be the father of a great nation. He wandered in the wilderness and became an archer.   —Bible, Gen. 16; 21:1–21. See also: Abraham; Isaac.

Israel When Jacob (second son and inheritor of Isaac and Rebekah) encountered an angel one day, they wrestled. The angel, who was unable to win the match in spite of his use of certain superhuman abilities, asked to be released. Jacob insisted that the angel bless him first, and he did, changing his name to Israel, which may mean "He strives with God." Israel was to become the patriarch of the nation of Israel; the twelve tribes of that nation were named for ten of his sons and two of his grandsons. This eminence had been foretold to Rebekah by God while Jacob was still in the womb and revealed to Jacob in a dream.   —Bible, Gen. 25:23; 28:10–15; 32:24–30; 41:50–52.

It is better to light one candle than curse the darkness. Rather than simply stew and complain in bitter futility about a gloomy situation, one ought to try to brighten it, if only a little bit.   —motto of the Christopher Society.

It is easier for a camel to go through the eye of a needle . . . . . . than for a rich man to enter into the kingdom of God. When a man asks what one should do in order to have eternal life, Jesus tells him to obey the Ten Commandments and sell all he has and give to the poor.   —Bible, Matt. 19:24.

It is finished. The last words of Jesus as he hung on the Cross. His mission consummated, ". . . he bowed his head, and gave up the ghost."   —Bible, John 19:30.

It is magnificent, but it is not war. The remark of a French general who witnessed the charge of the Light Brigade. He was impressed by the bravery and discipline of the cavalry brigade which charged to certain destruction, but objective enough to note that such a spectacular sacrifice of disciplined troops was militarily, tactically absurd.   —Pierre Bosquet.

it takes a thief   —See: to catch a thief.

It was the best of times, it was the worst of times.
The opening words of Charles Dickens's* novel, *A Tale of Two
Cities,* which tells a story set in the days of the French Revolution,
in the late 18th century. This remark could be made of almost any
era, of course—whether it is best or worst depends on the point of
view.

It's the only war we've got   Facetious response of an
American professional soldier to those who expressed doubt about
the wisdom or propriety of U.S. involvement in a foreign conflict.
It is as if to say, "It's better than nothing."

ivory tower   A place or state of mind in which the idealist or
the theorist is isolated from the real world. It is a tower in that he
takes refuge and fortifies himself there, high above it all; the fact
that it is ivory suggests that he considers his intellectual and artistic
preserve excellent, exclusive of mundane matters in the political
and   social   arenas.   —Charles   Augustin   Sainte-Beuve,
Pensées d'Aout.

J

J. Alfred Prufrock   Narrator of a poem by T. S. Eliot. Fussy and unsure of himself, a frequenter of salons and afternoon teas, Prufrock is painfully self-conscious and uncertain of how—or even whether—to speak to his blasé acquaintances of the quiet desperation and futility that he feels, for fear that he will make a fool of himself. Still, if he is unheroic and "a bit obtuse," at least he perceives the staleness and sterility of his life, which is more, one senses, than those around him do; at least he knows he is drowning.   —T. S. Eliot,* "The Love Song of J. Alfred Prufrock."

Jabberwocky   A poem, which consists largely of nonsense words, about a monstrous, mythical beast.   —Lewis Carroll,* *Through the Looking-Glass.*

Jacob   The second (by a matter of moments) of the twin sons born of Isaac and Rebekah. He and his brother Esau "struggled together within her" before birth, foreshadowing the contention between them in adulthood. Jacob's grasping of Esau's heel as Esau emerged from the womb before him seems to prefigure Jacob's overtaking Esau as their father's inheritor: when they were young men, Jacob extorted the rights to which Esau was entitled by his prior birth. With the help of Rebekah, who favored him,

Jacob disguised himself as his brother so that Isaac, whose eyes were failing, gave Jacob his first blessing.   —Bible, Gen. 25:21–34; 27:1–29.

Jacob's ladder   After offending his brother Esau, Jacob was sent away by his mother so that Esau could not kill him. At a place which he was to call Bethel, Jacob lay down to sleep, a stone for his pillow, and dreamed he saw a ladder reaching to heaven and angels going up and down it. At the top stood God, who told Jacob that he would be the father of a great nation which would live where Jacob now lay.   —Bible, Gen. 28:10–15.

Jarndyce vs. Jarndyce   The docket title of a court case in Charles Dickens's* novel *Bleak House.* This case is the classic example of what (Shakespeare's) Hamlet calls "the law's delay." As a result of repeated postponements and the maneuverings of the many parasitic attorneys who are involved, the case has grown like a cancer, or an unweeded garden, outliving many of the persons who have had a stake in it, becoming ever more tangled and complicated and choked with the documents that are the by-product of such a proceeding. When the suit is finally settled, the disputed funds over which it has been fought are gone, dissipated in court costs and lawyers' fees.

jawbone of an ass   —See: Samson.

J. B.   Title character in a verse drama (1958) by Archibald MacLeish, based on the biblical story of Job. The first and last letters of *Job* become the MacLeish character's first and second initials, used as a familiar but dignified form of address, as among businessmen.

Jehoshaphat There are five different characters in the Bible with this name, the most notable being the fourth king of Judah after the division of Solomon's kingdom. The name is commonly used as an exclamation.

Jekyll and Hyde Dr. Jekyll, who is good and kind, and Mr. Hyde, who is utterly evil, are actually the two personalities of one man, divided in Jekyll's experiment and alternately dominant. —Robert Louis Stevenson,* *The Strange Case of Doctor Jekyll and Mr. Hyde.*

Jephthah A great judge of Israel who vowed that he would sacrifice whatever he saw coming out of his house if God would deliver his enemies into his hands. After he won the battle, he returned to his home and saw his only daughter emerge to greet him. She sadly but piously acknowledged her father's obligation, and, heartsick, he paid it. —Bible, Judg. 11.

Jeremiah One of the three major prophets. He ringingly denounced immorality and superficial reformers and was at one time thought, erroneously, to be the author of the Book of Lamentations (the word means weeping and wailing); hence the coining of the word *jeremiad,* which is an extremely sad speech of denunciation.

Jeroboam First king of the Northern Kingdom after the division of Solomon's kingdom into Israel and Judah. He reverted to the

worship of the pagan god Baal and allowed other cults.
—Bible, I Kings 11:26–40; 12:1–20, 26–33.

Jerusalem   Chief city of Palestine, held sacred by Christians, Jews, and Moslems; Zion; the City of David; site of Solomon's Temple; capital of Israel (and, after the division of the Kingdom, of Judah); footstool of the heavenly Jerusalem of the Book of Revelation.

Jew of Tarsus   Thus St. Paul identifies himself to the captain who is taking him to the Roman fortress in Jerusalem. The captain suspects him of being an Egyptian who has fomented recent disturbances in the city, but when he hears that Paul is a Roman citizen (Tarsus was in the province of Cilicia), he gives him an opportunity to explain.   —Bible, Acts 21:39.

Jezebel   Wicked wife of Ahab, King of Israel. She influenced him to worship the pagan god Baal, brought prophets of that cult into the court and persecuted the prophets of God, particularly Elijah, having many of them killed. Her evil is further exemplified by the way she acquired a man's vineyard for her husband, conspiring to have the fellow falsely accused of blasphemy so that he was stoned to death. She died horribly, as was prophesied.   —Bible, I Kings 16:30–33; 18:6–19; 21:1–16; II Kings 9:10; 30–37.

Jim Crow   An insulting reference to American blacks. The term first appeared in an anonymous song dating from the early 1880's; in later years it came to refer to regulations, laws, etc. in effect in the South which prohibit blacks from enjoying the same privileges as white people.

Job   In order to prove to Satan that Job was absolutely faithful and upright, God permitted Satan to cause Job every kind of affliction short of death. Although he was bewildered, and complained at one point that he wished he had never been born, Job proved his faith in God by humbly submitting to God's will.

John Brown's body   . . . lies a-moldering in the grave,/His soul is marching on.   In 1859 the abolitionist zealot John Brown seized a federal arsenal at Harper's Ferry, Virginia, intending to incite a rebellion of slaves. He was captured and hanged, but he marched on in spirit before the armies that fought to free the slaves in the Civil War of 1861–1865. American author Stephen Vincent Benét wrote a long narrative poem about the Civil War entitled *John Brown's Body* (1928).   —Thomas Brigham Bishop, "John Brown's Body."

John Bull   The symbol of Great Britain, represented by a short, stout, middle-aged gentleman. The origin of the name is unknown, but as early as 1712 it appeared in Dr. John Arbuthnot's *Law is a Bottomless Pit,* later republished as *The History of John Bull.*

John the Baptist   An ascetic mystic and reformer of priestly descent, related to Jesus, who meditated in the wilderness and baptized those who came to him, immersing them in the Jordan River as a ritual cleansing. He heralded the coming of Christ, who submitted to John's baptism. Like Christ, he was considered a dangerous rabble-rouser by the conservative religious establishment; he was ultimately beheaded.

Johnny Get Your Gun   A lively song of encouragement to the citizen soldier, set to a jig tune. George M. Cohan incorporated a

portion of it in his famous song "Over There," of World War I
vintage.   —Monroe H. Rosenfeld (1884).

Jonah   A jinx; a person who supposedly brings bad luck wherever
he goes. Jonah's presence on board a ship was thought to be the
reason it was almost wrecked in a storm. The men threw Jonah into
the sea, where he was swallowed by a large fish. After three days
and nights, the fish released Jonah.

Joseph   Son of Jacob, he became the servant of one of Pharaoh's
officers. This man's wife accused him falsely, and he was imprisoned. Two of Pharaoh's servants were imprisoned with him, and he
correctly interpreted their dreams. One was later released and told
Pharaoh that Joseph could interpret Pharaoh's dream. He did so,
and was given great power. Joseph prepared for the famine that
Pharaoh's dream had forecast. When it struck, his father and
brothers, among many other people, came to Egypt for food. They
were all reunited and lived in the land of Goshen. There they
multiplied, and the families of ten of Jacob's sons and two
grandsons (by Joseph) became the Twelve Tribes of the People of
Israel.   —Bible, Gen. 39—50.   See also: coat of many colors.

jot or a tittle   *Iota* is the ninth and smallest letter of the Greek
alphabet, in Latin *iota* or *jota;* thus an iota or a jot is the very tiniest
amount. A tittle is a small mark used in printing to indicate
pronunciation of a letter or combination of letters in a word; it also
denotes a small amount.   —Bible, Matt. 5:18.

joy in the morning   The psalmist praises God for his mercy
—"his anger endureth but a moment," and while a man may weep

for a night, "joy cometh in the morning."   —Bible, Psalm 30:5.

Judas   Judas Iscariot was one of the Twelve Apostles. Perhaps disappointed to find that Jesus was not to come to power as a worldly ruler, Judas became disenchanted with him and betrayed him to the priests; this led to Jesus' crucifixion.   —Bible, Matt. 26.   See also: kiss of death; thirty pieces of silver.

Judgment Day   The day on which the principle of punishment for sin and reward for virtue will be carried out. This principle is enunciated throughout the Bible. Usually this term denotes the sudden, cataclysmic and spectacular drama depicted in the dream-vision of St. John the Divine: the dead standing before God on his throne as in a cosmic courtroom; Jesus' examination of the books which presumably list those deemed worthy of eternal life or damnation; the descent of the heavenly Jerusalem, and the entrance thereinto of the saints; and the relegation of sinners to "the lake which burneth with fire and brimstone: which is the second death."   —Bible, Rev. 20—22.

just growed   Topsy, a little slave girl in pre-Civil War times, claims that she has no knowledge of having been born. "I 'spect," she says, "I grow'd."   —Harriet Beecher Stowe,* *Uncle Tom's Cabin.*

just and the unjust   In his Sermon on the Mount, Jesus admonishes the people not to strike back at their enemies, but to love them so "That ye may be the children of your Father," who causes the sun to shine on the evil and the good "and sendeth rain on the just and the unjust" alike.   —Bible, Matt. 5:45.

justify the ways of God to man, to   —See: *Paradise Lost.*

K

Katzenjammer Kids   Two mischievous boys, Hans and Fritz, featured in the comic strip of the same name, begun in the 1890's by Rudolf Dirks. In German, *Katzenjammer* means "hangover"—literally, "a disturbance of cats" (in one's head), which is a graphic description of what a hangover feels like.

keys of the kingdom   Jesus, addressing his apostle Peter, who had just stated his belief that Jesus was the Son of God, told Peter that he would give him the keys of the kingdom of heaven. It is generally presumed that Jesus meant that he would show Peter (and other loyal believers) the means by which they could some day enter heaven. Scottish author A.J. Cronin wrote a novel called *The Keys of the Kingdom* in 1941.   —Bible, Matt. 16:19.

kill the fatted calf   To make someone very welcome, literally by serving him a meal of the animal which has been set aside and well-fed to make a feast.   —Bible, Luke 15:23.   See also: prodigal son.

kill with kindness To be excessively thoughtful and considerate. Usually there is really no question of the recipient's being harmed in any way by such treatment; the term simply denotes the ultimate in charity.   —William Shakespeare, *The Taming of the Shrew*, act 4, sc. 1.

killing the goose that laid the golden eggs Destroying the source of one's good fortune. A man had a goose which laid eggs of pure gold. Greedily intent on getting all the golden eggs at once, he killed the goose, and found nothing inside.   —Aesop,* "The Goose with the Golden Eggs."

King Arthur Historically, Arthur was a British chieftain in the 6th century who fought many battles against the Anglo-Saxon invaders and became king of a tribe of ancient Britons called the Silures. Over the years, many different versions of his life have appeared by authors such as Sir Thomas Malory* (*Morte d'Arthur*), Alfred, Lord Tennyson* (*Idylls of the King*), and T. H. White (*The Once and Future King*). The popular musical by Alan Jay Lerner and Frederick Loewe, *Camelot*, is also based on the stories of King Arthur. In all of these romances, Arthur and his loyal retainers are depicted as armored knights of a much later period (12th—14th centuries) who lived and fought according to the idealistic traditions of medieval chivalry.

King James Bible King James I of England commissioned a group of scholars to translate the Bible into English. They finished the work in 1611, and since then this version has been known as the King James Bible.

King Lear   Central figure in William Shakespeare's tragedy of the same name. King of ancient Britain, Lear abdicated in his old age in favor of his three daughters. In apportioning his kingdom, he foolishly made the share each daughter would receive contingent upon her verbal expression of love for him. The two older daughters complied glibly (and insincerely); the youngest daughter's reply, although heartfelt, was not extravagant enough to suit him, and he disinherited her; this he lived to regret.

Kingmaker   The Kingmaker was Richard Neville, Earl of Warwick (1449–1471), a very influential, energetic and ambitious man who fought for the Yorkists against the Lancastrians at the beginning of the Wars of the Roses; he was largely responsible for putting Edward, Duke of York, on the throne as Edward IV. Later, when Edward did not do as Warwick wished, he supported the Lancastrians and restored Henry VI to the throne. Thus a kingmaker is one who uses his influence to bring a party's leader to power, whether by war or political manipulation, and may expect to benefit his own ends as a result.

kiss and tell   To have an amorous relationship and tell others about it afterwards.   —William Congreve,* *Love for Love.*

kiss of death   The original kiss of death was given by Judas Iscariot to Jesus in the Garden of Gethsemane. Judas had agreed to betray his master Jesus to the priests for thirty pieces of silver; he told them he would identify Jesus by kissing him. This he did, and "they . . . laid hands on Jesus and took him;" and he was crucified the next day. Thus a kiss of death is a display of love, friendship, support, or simply association which, whatever the purpose, has a harmful effect.   —Bible, Matt. 26:47–50.

kiss of Judas   —See: kiss of death.

knew not, eating death, and   The poet describes the climactic and fatal moment when Eve, succumbing to the subtle, persuasive blandishments of the serpent, eats the forbidden fruit. In an access of pride, rapt with pleasure, she does not realize that this act will result in the loss of Paradise, in her death and that of all her descendants.   —John Milton,* *Paradise Lost.*

. . . knew not Joseph.   The children of Israel, brought to Egypt by their brother Joseph with the blessing of the pharaoh whom Joseph served, multiplied over the generations. A new king came to the throne of Egypt; he did not feel any obligation to the Israelites, and thereafter the Egyptians persecuted them and made them slaves.   —Bible, Exod. 1:7–14.   See also: Joseph; Moses.

knight-errant   Most knights were beholden to their lords and must always be prepared to serve them. A knight-errant (the term suggests wandering or straying) was what might be called a freelance knight who sought his own quests and operated independently.

Knight of the Woeful/Rueful Countenance   Don Quixote, the self-styled knight-errant who is repeatedly frustrated in his attempts to assert his chivalrous ideals; he dies in disillusionment.   —Miguel de Cervantes.*

Knightly Quest   A gallant and chivalrous expedition to achieve, by force of arms, some high and worthy purpose: to rescue a lady in distress, as the Red Cross Knight does in Edmund

Spenser's* epic poem *The Faerie Queene* (1590—1596); to take the Holy Land from the Saracen infidels, as the Crusaders set out to do; to obtain the Holy Grail, as Sir Galahad did.

Know thyself Inscription on the Delphic oracle in ancient Greece. At Delphi, it was believed, gods spoke through the lips of the priestess, revealing their knowledge and divine purposes. The priestess' pronouncements were usually obscure and ambiguous, and this inscription probably gave those who came to consult the oracle the best advice they could hope for—which, if followed, might make oracles unnecessary. Certainly, one who wishes to know anything ought properly to begin by attempting to know himself (which is more difficult than it sounds).   —Plutarch,* *Morals.*

Kubla Khan The 13th century founder of the Mongol dynasty in China. The poet describes his erection of a marvelous palace in Xanadu.   —Samuel Taylor Coleridge,* "Kubla Khan."

Kurtz —See: (The) horror! The horror!

L

La Belle Dame Sans Merci "The beautiful lady without mercy"—a lovely "faery's child" celebrated in a ballad by John

Keats,* she enthralls a knight-at-arms, as she has enthralled kings and princes before him, and cruelly leaves him "Alone and Palely loitering."

labor of love   Work which one is devoted to and thoroughly enjoys doing, for the sake of the work itself rather than any material compensation; originally, the work of faith performed by members of the early Church.   —Bible, I Thess. 1:3.

labors of Hercules   Hercules, a brave, strong hero of Greek myth, was given twelve immensely difficult tasks to accomplish, such as killing the many-headed Hydra; capturing the Cretan bull; and bringing the three-headed dog Cerberus up from the underworld. He accomplished all these feats.

Lady April   The poet personifies April as a fair damsel with all the sweet, fresh attributes of nature in the early spring. She radiates hope, but there are "Traces of tears [on] her languid lashes" because, the poet suggests, she foresees the "withered leaves" of autumn, "And winter bringing end in barrenness." —Ernest Dowson,* "My Lady April."

Lady Chatterley   Heroine of the story of a married woman who consorts with the gamekeeper on her estate. The novel was long banned because of its explicit depiction of the sexual act in plain and earthy language, through which the author expresses his distaste for social hypocrisy and society's high regard for intellect at the expense of passion.   —D. H. Lawrence,* *Lady Chatterley's Lover.*

Lady Godiva English countess of the 11th century who, according to folklore, begged her husband to remit the heavy taxes he had levied on the town of Coventry. He said he would if she agreed to ride through the town nude. This may have been an ironic way of saying that he would never do it, but she took him at his word and made the journey, first letting down her long hair to conceal most of her nakedness. It was said that everyone remained indoors with their windows shuttered, but that a fellow named Tom succumbed to the temptation to peep.

Lady of the Lake In Arthurian legend, the lady ("clothed in white samite, mystic, wonderful," according to Tennyson*) who lives in a lake. She is the mother or foster mother of Lancelot du Lac. According to one version of the story, it is she who gives Arthur his magic sword Excalibur, and it is to her that Arthur has the sword returned just before his death. In the poem by Sir Walter Scott,* the Lady of the Lake is the daughter of Lord Douglas, who lives by Loch Katrine.

"Lady or the Tiger?, The" The title of Frank R. Stockton's short story about a young man who must make a fateful choice between two doors: one conceals a man-eating tiger, the other conceals a lovely girl. Which will he choose? The author leaves it up to the reader to decide.

Lamb, The So Jesus was described by John the Baptist. —Bible, John 1:29; Rev. 5–18.

lamb to the slaughter, like a In a ritual sacrifice, a pure and innocent "victim"—a lamb, for example—would be killed

and offered to the deity. Being innocent, it would have the capacity to take on, symbolically, the sins of those who offered it; thus they would be cleansed and the deity satisfied, not only with the savor of the burned flesh which rose to him but with the offerer's expiation of his sin. When the prophet uses this phrase he is referring to the expected Messiah, who will be killed as a supreme sacrifice upon whom "the Lord hath laid . . . the iniquity of us all."
—Bible, Isa. 53:7.

lamp unto my feet   The psalmist says that the Lord's word lights his way through life like a lamp that prevents him from stumbling in the dark.   —Bible, Ps. 119:105.

Lancelot   One of the best-known knights of King Arthur's Round Table. He was brave and much admired, but his affair with Queen Guinevere led to the ruin of both the lovers.

land flowing with milk and honey, a   God promised Moses that he would lead the Jews into a land of plenty, overflowing with good things.   —Bible, Exod. 33:1–3.

land of Goshen   Formerly used as a mild oath or expression of surprise. The land of Goshen was a region in northeastern Egypt. Here Joseph, Pharaoh's prime minister, directed that his father Jacob and Jacob's other sons be settled, and here Joseph drove out in his chariot to greet them. Later, the Exodus of the Jews passed through this region.   —Bible, Gen. 45:10.

land of Nod   The place "on the east of Eden" where Cain went to live after God exiled him. The phrase has come to mean

"sleep."   —Bible, Gen. 4:16.   See also: Cain; east of Eden;
mark of Cain; my brother's keeper.

last Adam   St. Paul tells the faithful of Corinth that ". . . the
first man Adam was made a living soul; the last Adam was made a
quickening spirit"—i.e., a spirit which comes alive. He means that
in the beginning Adam was created a natural (physical) body, and
that body decomposed in death; in the end Adam will be
resurrected in another form—as a seed which is sown in the earth
is altered by its interment, and the grain which grows from it does
not have the same "body" as that seed; yet they are one.
—Bible, I Cor. 15:45.

last ditch   The last foxhole, trench, or other defensible position
in which a soldier may make a stand against the enemy.
—King William III.

last hurrah   From the title of a novel (1956) by Edwin
O'Connor about Boston mayoral politics. The central figure is a
shrewd Irish machine politician of humble origin who has to fight
hidebound Back Bay conservatives. (They resent his power and
popularity and frankly high-handed methods, although he is really
quite a good mayor.) The title suggests, as well as the end of his
career, the excitement, hoopla, and smoke-filled rooms of
old-style campaigning.

Last Judgment   According to the dream-vision of St. John the
Divine, after the millennium—the thousand years of Christ's reign
on earth after his second coming—Satan will be released from
hell, defeated utterly in his battle against Christ and cast into hell

forever. Then all the dead will be resurrected and judged "according to their works," and whoever is not "found written in the book of life" will be "cast into the lake of fire."   —Bible, Rev. 20.

last of the Mohicans   In James Fenimore Cooper's* novel (1826), the last surviving members of the Mohican tribe are Chingachgook and his son Uncas. Uncas is usually referred to as the last of the Mohicans, but he dies during the course of the story, leaving his father as the last remaining Mohican.

last refuge of a scoundrel   Samuel Johnson* stated that patriotism (presumably insincere patriotism) is the last refuge of a scoundrel—i.e., the last excuse he can find to shield him from criticism for his behavior.   —James Boswell,* *Life of Johnson.*

last straw   The last straw is the one that breaks the camel's back, the one infinitesimal burden added to the others already accumulated that drives one to the breaking point.

Last Supper, the   At the last meal shared by Jesus and his followers prior to his arrest, he announced that one of the Twelve Apostles seated there with him would betray him. Judas Iscariot did so almost immediately after this meal. (The most famous painting of this scene is by Leonardo da Vinci.)   —Bible, Matt. 26:17–29.

law is a ass   Mr. Bumble, upon being told that the law

considers a man to be responsible for his wife's behavior, replies that, if that is so, "the law is a ass, a idiot!"—as if "the law" were a person. He also assumes "the law" to be a bachelor.
—Charles Dickens,* *Oliver Twist.*

law's delay   In Hamlet's soliloquy beginning "To be, or not to be," the hero lists the many things in life which he finds hard to bear or to live with. "The law's delay" is one of them.
—William Shakespeare, *Hamlet,* act 3, sc. 1. See also: Jarndyce vs. Jarndyce.

lay on, Macduff   Confronted by his nemesis Macduff, Macbeth boldly invites him to strike with all the vigor he can summon, adding that whichever of them first asks for quarter may be damned as far as he is concerned.   —William Shakespeare, *Macbeth,* act 5, sc. 8.

laying on of hands   Bringing about the miraculous healing of illness, spiritual as well as divine, by means of touching. Jesus performed such cures, and he commissioned his apostles to do so.   —Bible, Matt. 9:23–35; 10:1.

Lazarus   A man (brother of Mary and Martha of Bethany) whom Jesus raised from the dead.   —Bible, John 11:1–44.

Le Morte d'Arthur   A well-known treatment of the legends of King Arthur written by Sir Thomas Malory* in the late 15th century.

lean and hungry look   Catching a glimpse of his supposedly loyal general Cassius, Julius Caesar is disturbed. It occurs to him that Cassius' emaciated features suggest a hunger for something other than food—advancement, perhaps. "He thinks too much," muses Caesar: "such men are dangerous." As it turns out, Cassius does conspire to kill him.   —William Shakespeare, *Julius Caesar,* act 1, sc. 2.

leave her to heaven   The ghost of Prince Hamlet's father reveals to Hamlet that he was murdered by his brother, the present King, who is now married to Hamlet's mother. (Marriage to a brother-in-law constituted adultery.) The ghost tells Hamlet that no matter what he does about his uncle, he should not think of punishing his mother, but "Leave her to heaven"—i.e., God will see to her punishment. A novel entitled *Leave Her to Heaven* was written by Ben Ames Williams in 1944.   —William Shakespeare, *Hamlet,* act 1, sc. 5.

leave not a rack behind   The enchanter Prospero magically creates a pageant of spirits and then dissolves it with a word, observing as he does so that "the great globe itself" will also vanish without a trace one day.   —William Shakespeare, *Tempest,* act 4, sc. 1.

lebensraum   German: "living space." A term used by Adolf Hitler to designate the territory outside Germany which must be conquered if the German people were not to be stifled.

Left Bank   The left side of the River Seine when one faces downstream—i.e., the south side. The Bohemian quarter of Paris, inhabited by writers and artists with an unconventional way of life, is on the Left Bank of the river. It is roughly equivalent to New York's Greenwich Village.

left hand does not know what the right hand is doing, the   This often denotes a failure to coordinate the activities of an organization—one unit operates independent of and with no regard for the operation of another, and the result is a confused rather than a concentrated effort. Originally, Jesus used the image to describe the way alms should be given to the poor: "Let not thy left hand know what thy right hand doeth"—that is, practice charity privately, disinterestedly, and without making a display of it.   —Bible, Matt. 6:3.

left hand of God   Traditionally, the right hand of God is a place of favor; a great many passages in the Bible suggest this (e.g., Psalm 139: ". . . thy right hand shall hold me."). Although nothing sinister could be attributed to God, presumably one who is at God's left hand or with whom God deals left-handedly is somewhat disreputable or flawed.   See also: sinister.

left-handed compliment   A compliment which, because of the way in which it is worded, seems insincere or inadequate.   See also: damn with faint praise; sinister.

leper colony   A more or less remote enclave where victims of leprosy (Hansen's disease) are isolated from those not infected. Lepers have been excluded not only to prevent communication of the disease (in fact, it is not very contagious) but also because others found the deformities it often causes so repugnant.

Figuratively, a leper colony is a state or condition of separation from the mainstream of society because of any acts or expressions which make one "untouchable."

l'etat c'est moi   —See: I am the state.

let George do it   "Don't look at me; let somebody else do it." The expression can be traced back as for as King Louis XII of France.

let me count the ways.   That is, let me list all the different ways in which "I love thee."   —Elizabeth Barrett Browning,* *Sonnets from the Portuguese,* No. 43.

Let my people go.   Thus Moses and Aaron, spokesmen for God, address Pharaoh on behalf of God's chosen people, the Israelites, whom the Egyptians hold in bondage.   —Bible, Exod. 5:1.

let the chips fall where they may   A woodsman who concentrates on his chopping does not care where the chips fall. By the same token, a man who is intent on doing a good job of any kind is not concerned about inconveniencing those who may stand in the way and impede his work. If he is President of the United States, for example, he will not hesitate to let the chips fall on the special interest groups that profit by the conditions he seeks to alter.   —Roscoe Conkling, speech nominating President Grant for a third term.   See also: hew to the line.

Let sleeping dogs lie. Persons, situations, or issues which may prove troublesome if aroused are better left undisturbed. —Charles Dickens,* *David Copperfield.*

Let them eat cake. This was the bland reply of a princess (evidently not Marie Antoinette of France, to whom it is usually attributed) when she was told that the poor people had no bread. She seems actually to have believed they had a choice. Thus it is the classic expression of an aristocrat's utter failure to appreciate the problems of the poor. Because he has always been insulated from them, he finds the idea of need completely foreign.   —Jean Jacques Rousseau, *Les Confessions.*

Let this cup pass from me. The cup contains the suffering and death that Jesus knows he must swallow the next day when he will be taken by the priests and scourged and crucified by the Romans. In the Garden of Gethsemane, Jesus' human heart almost fails him as he contemplates the morrow, and he asks God, "if it be possible," to spare him that. Then he adds, ". . . nevertheless, not as I will, but as thou wilt."   —Bible, Matt. 26:39

Let us now praise famous men . . . and our fathers that begat us. It is fitting that those who have made names for themselves be glorified. In 1941, James Agee, American film critic and novelist, wrote a book called *Let Us Now Praise Famous Men.*   —Apocrypha: Eccles. 44:1.

leviathan A large, powerful seagoing creature, thought by many to represent a whale, but referred to by Isaiah as a

"crooked serpent . . . the dragon that is in the sea."
—Bible, Job 41:1; Isa. 27:1.

liberal arts The arts in question—the so-called humanities—are liberal in the sense that they are bountiful and also in the sense that they offer freedom from baseness, ignorance, and authoritarianism. The enchanter Prospero, deposed Duke of Milan, figuratively demonstrates the power that reason and the love of books afford. He uses this term when telling his daughter of his commitment to the study which has made him what he is—sure and knowing, but also tolerant and broadminded—a man superbly in control of flesh and spirit and of his own destiny.   —William Shakespeare, *The Tempest,* act 1, sc. 2.

Lie down with dogs . . . . . . and you will get up with fleas. That is, if you lower yourself to associate with persons of dubious reputation, you must expect to be contaminated by them.   —George Herbert,* *Jacula Prudentum.*

life which is unexamined is not worth living, the Every man is obliged rationally to study and reflect on the nature and purpose of his existence so that he will live in such a way as to fulfill his humanity, rather than merely survive as beasts do. According to Plato, Socrates believed that the *psyche* (soul or intellect or life principle) is immortal and capable of achieving wisdom—of knowing what he called the Good—after death, but only if one suppresses bodily appetites and strives to gain knowledge. Moreover, he maintained that if anyone could prove that his conclusions were wrong, he would alter them accordingly; he was constantly examining his life in an effort to know the truth.   —Plato, *The Apology.*

Life-in-Death A morbid state of semi-existence experienced by a seaman who is responsible for the suffering of his shipmates. Delirious with thirst, he imagines that a ghastly woman—"Her lips were red, her looks were free,/Her locks were yellow as gold./Her skin was as white as leprosy,/The Nightmare Life-in-Death was she . . ."—is casting dice with Death as her skeletal ship comes alongside. The stakes in the game are the lives of the seaman and his shipmates; the woman wins him, and the rest of his crew perish.   —Samuel Taylor Coleridge,* "The Rime of the Ancient Mariner."

lift me as a wave, a leaf, a cloud The poet, "chained and bowed" by the crass, mundane, and moribund preoccupations of society, calls upon the West Wind to raise him above that and "Drive [his] dead thoughts over the universe/Like withered leaves to quicken a new birth . . ."   —Percy Bysshe Shelley,* "Ode to the West Wind."

lift oneself by one's own bootstraps In times when boots were more common than shoes, they were often equipped with straps, protruding from the top, which were grasped to pull the boots on. It is, of course, impossible to pick oneself up with those; the term is an extravagantly exaggerated figure of speech for advancing one's position all by oneself, without anyone else's help.

light of perverted science "Light" in the sense of discovery; "perverted" because its purpose is destruction rather than advancement. In a neat paradox, the speaker sees that the triumph of Nazi Germany would mean the coming of ". . . a new Dark Age, made more sinister and perhaps more protracted . . ."

by the dedication of scientific discovery to such corrupt uses as military ordnance.   —Winston Churchill,* speech in the House of Commons on the day France surrendered to Germany.

light under a bushel   In the Sermon on the Mount, Jesus tells his disciples that they are "the light of the world," for they know and believe in him. Thus they should "Let [their] light so shine before men that they may see [the disciples'] good works." Jesus implies that he would no more have given them the light of understanding if they were not to use it than a man would light a candle in order to shed light and then conceal it under a basket.   —Bible, Matt. 5:15.

lilies of the field   Jesus tells how beautiful the lilies are, pointing out that even though they don't do any work, God provides handsomely for them. Thus God will provide even more for men.   —Bible, Matt. 6:28.

lilliputian   Extremely small; tiny. The fictitious land of Lilliput, one of those countries visited by Lemuel Gulliver, was inhabited by little people about six inches tall.   —Jonathan Swift,* *Gulliver's Travels.*

lion is in the streets, a   The excuse offered by a lazy man for his failure to be up and about. A novel called *A Lion in the Streets,* written by Adria Locke Langley, was published in 1945. —Bible, Prov. 26:13.

Lion of Judah   In the dream-vision of St. John the Divine, Christ is referred to as "the Lion of the tribe of Judah, the Root of David," although he appears here as a Lamb with seven horns and seven eyes.   —Bible, Rev. 5:5—6.

lion's share   The lion, together with three other animals, caught a stag. They were going to divide it into equal shares, but the lion, being the most ferocious of the four, decided that all four shares rightly belonged to him. Therefore, the lion's share of anything is not the largest part, but *all* of it.   —Aesop's* *Fables*.

Little Boy Blue   Eugene Field's* poignant poem about a beloved child who dies and whose toys remain, forlornly moldering, where he left them. "Little boy blue" also refers to the wayward shepherd boy of the nursery rhyme who sleeps under a haystack while sheep roam the meadow and cows eat the corn.

. . . and a little child shall lead them   The prophet proclaims the coming of the Messiah, who will bring righteousness and peace to the world. In that day predatory and domestic animals will lie down together, and even a little child shall be able to tend all such animals without fear of being devoured. —Bible, Isa. 11:6.

little corporal   Napoleon Bonaparte, who gained this nickname after the 1796 battle of Lodi, because of his youthful age and five-foot-two-inch height.

Little Lord Fauntleroy   Seven-year-old hero of Frances Hodgson Burnett's 1886 story of the same name. Because he was dressed in black velvet with a lace collar and had blond curls, the name has come to refer to a spoiled or effeminate small boy.

little lower than the angels, a   So God made man; and so, says St. Paul, God made Jesus (although, as God's Son, he was "so much better than the angels") in order that Jesus "might be a merciful . . . priest . . . to make reconciliation for the sins of the people."   —Bible, Heb. 2:7.

live high on the hog   To live well, presumably in that one can afford to eat those cuts of the animal which are higher and therefore more expensive than, say, the feet and hocks.

live off the land   To eat only that food which comes to hand in a wilderness area—wild animals, berries, roots, etc.—without recourse to processed or artificial nutrients.

loaves and fishes   When Jesus told his disciples to feed the crowd of five thousand who had followed him, they protested that they had only five loaves of bread and two fishes. Jesus then blessed that food and broke it, and all five thousand were fed, with twelve baskets left over. A nearly identical miracle is recorded in the very next chapter.   —Bible, Matt. 14:15–21; 15:32–38.

lock, stock and barrel   The reference is to a rifle, specifically a flintlock musket. If you sell something in its entirety, you sell it lock (the firing mechanism), stock (the wooden shoulder butt), and barrel—there isn't anything else.

locusts and wild honey   The austere food eaten by John the Baptist during the time he preached and baptized in the wilderness. Apparently he lived off the land, sustaining himself on very humble fare which was in keeping with his rough and simple garments of camel hair.   —Bible, Matt. 3:4.

Lolita   Title heroine of Vladimir Nabokov's novel (1955) about a middle-aged professor, Humbert Humbert, who is smitten and obsessed by twelve-year-old Lolita's adolescent beauty.

look homeward, Angel   Addressing his dead friend, now an angel, the poet asks him to look back with pity on those who, mourning, have been left behind. Used as the title of a novel (1929) by Thomas Wolfe.*   —John Milton,* *Lycidas*.

looking-glass war   When Alice (of Wonderland fame) goes through the looking-glass, she finds herself in a world where everything, including people, is a mirror image of itself in the real world. Needless to say, she finds this very confusing for it is difficult to know how to behave and what is what. The cold war of espionage is like that—it is a war of deception and double agents, and appearances are not to be trusted. Used as the title of a novel (1965) by John Le Carré.

looking-glass world   A fantastic dream world where everything is a reversed or mirror (looking-glass) image of the real world.   —Lewis Carroll,* *Through the Looking-Glass*.   See also: Never-Never Land; Wonderland.

lord of the flies   From time to time, the Israelites lost faith in God and worshipped the false gods of Canaan and Palestine. One of these gods was Baalzebub ("lord of flies" in Canaanite). Jesus and his contemporaries refer to him as Beelzebub. In *Paradise Lost,* John Milton* names Satan's lieutenant Beelzebub. In *The Pilgrim's Progress,* John Bunyan refers to Satan as Beelzebub. Title of a novel (1954) by William Golding.   —Bible, II Kings 1.   See also: golden calf.

Lord gave, and the Lord hath taken away, the   This is Job's initial reaction to the suffering and loss which God permits Satan to inflict upon him to test his faith. Job piously and philosophically observes that what God has seen fit to give him, God is certainly entitled to take away, and it is not Job's place to ask why. He concludes his statement with the words ". . . blessed be the name of the Lord."   —Bible, Job 1:21.

lost generation   A term coined by American (expatriate) poet, novelist, and critic Gertrude Stein. It refers to that generation of primarily Americans and Englishmen which was young enough to participate (actually or vicariously) in World War I, and old enough to be embittered and disillusioned by the experience. Because of the appalling loss of life that war caused, and the dismal, dreary, and banal circumstances under which it was fought, it became difficult or impossible to believe in God and entertain romantic, idealistic, or even merely optimistic expectations of the social system.

Lotos-Eaters, the   The *lotophagi,* those people of ancient Greek legend who ate the fruit of the lotos tree, which was supposed to induce a state of dreamy indolence, irresponsibility and forgetfulness of home. The Greeks who accompanied Ulysses (Odysseus) in his ten years' wandering after the Trojan War came to Lotos Land and were tempted by lotos-eaters to taste the fruit and remain.

Lot's wife   Lot, a good man, lived in a wicked city. God, intending to destroy the wicked city, sent angels to lead Lot and his family away. They were told not to look back; his wife did and was turned into a pillar of salt.   —Bible, Gen. 19:1–26.   See also: Abraham.

lov'd, not wisely, but too well   Othello, persuaded by Iago that his wife has been unfaithful, kills her and then discovers that Iago was lying. In an agony of remorse, he asks to be remembered as "one that lov'd, not wisely, but too well," and then he stabs himself.   —William Shakespeare, *Othello*, act 5, sc. 2.

"Love Among the Ruins"   Title of a poem by Robert Browning* about a shepherd, grazing his flock on a site reminiscent of the glory of ancient Rome, long since vanished, who reflects on the impermanence of such things; and, in the knowledge that "a girl with eager eyes" awaits him where Caesar watched the chariots, he concludes that "Love is best."

loved I not honor more   A dashing, gallant, and romantic cavalier, off to pursue "a new mistress"—the enemy on some distant field of battle—assures the girl he leaves behind that his "inconstancy" to her is not unkind; for he could not love her as much as he does if he did not love honor more.   —Richard Lovelace,* "To Lucasta, Going to the Wars."

Lucifer   An archangel who rebelled against God. When he was cast out of Heaven into Hell, he became known as Satan, the Devil.   —Bible, Isa. 14:12.   See also: Satan.

Lucullan   Pertaining to the delights of fine and luxurious dining. The word is a reference to Lucullus, the Roman general and consul who lived from roughly 110 to about 57 B.C., and who became widely known for his wealth and lavish banquets.

M

mad as a hatter or a March hare   In Wonderland, Alice has tea with a Hatter and a March Hare. It is a wild affair because these two are more eccentric than most inhabitants of Wonderland. In the 19th century, some hatmakers apparently did sustain damage to the brain or nervous system because of exposure to mercury, which was used to treat the felt from which the hats were made. The proverbial madness of March hares goes back at least as far as the English poet John Skelton (1460–1529), and derives from the frantic behavior of the animal, which is in a state of sexual excitement at that time of year.   —Lewis Carroll,* *Alice in Wonderland.*

mad dogs and Englishmen   According to the song, the only creatures crazy enough to be outdoors in the broiling midday sun are "mad dogs and Englishmen." The song is written from the point of view of one of Britain's former colonials, living in the tropics, where the noonday sun can cause heat prostration. This did not deter the pith-helmeted English, who insisted on adhering to the same schedule that they had followed in northern Europe, while the natives retreated from the punishing heat.   —Noel Coward, "Mad Dogs and Englishmen."

Madame Bovary   Heroine of the 1856 novel of the same name by French author Gustav Flaubert. Emma Bovary was married to a dull-witted village doctor, had dreams of romance and several lovers, accumulated large debts, and eventually killed herself. The book is considered one of the first novels of the realistic school.

madder music   In a desperate attempt to forget his lost love, the poet calls for strong wine and wild music; "but when the feast is finished" her shadow falls across his thoughts again.   —Ernest Dowson,* "Non Sum Qualis Eram Bonae Sub Regno Cynarae."

made in Japan   A phrase which was synonymous with cheapness and sleaziness prior to World War II, when products stamped with that legend were very common. It has come to have a very ironic ring in the 1970's and 1980's, of course, because of the many high-quality products, made in Japan, that have enabled her to become so preeminent in world commerce.

Magdalene   Mary Magdalene was, traditionally, a harlot ". . . out of whom [Jesus] had cast seven devils." She followed him, stood by the Cross, attended his burial, and was one of the first to see the open tomb and the risen Jesus.   —Bible, Mark 15:40, 47; 16:1–9; John 20:1–18.

magus   A magician or sorcerer; the plural is *magi,* by which name the wise men from the East, who brought gifts to the infant Jesus, are often identified. *The Magus* (1966; rev. 1977), by English novelist John Fowles, is about a mysterious man of modern times who stages elaborate illusions on an island off the coast of Greece.

make haste slowly   This seemingly self-contradictory expression means that one should use discretion and care, even when attempting to accomplish something in a hurry. Augustus Caesar (63 B.C.—A.D. 14) said: "More haste, less speed," meaning that if one is merely hasty he will not get finished any faster, because too many mistakes will have to be corrected.   —Greek proverb.

make a virtue of necessity   To delude oneself or others with the pretense that the beneficial act one has performed was deliberate and therefore virtuous, when in fact it was something that *had* to be done and therefore really does one no credit. The expression may also mean "to make the best of a bad situation."   —Quintilian,* *Institutiones Oratoriae.*

make the world safe for democracy   Asking Congress to declare war against the Central Powers in 1917, President Woodrow Wilson said, "The world must be made safe for democracy."

malapropism   —See: Mrs. Malaprop.

man doth not live by bread only   This statement is often taken out of context and used in such a way as to suggest that, in addition to hunger for food, man has other appetites. This is true, of course, but originally Moses meant that in addition to *all* of his appetites, man has a need for ". . . every word that proceedeth out of the mouth of the Lord." Jesus echoes this principle in the New Testament.   —Bible, Deut. 8:3.

man Friday   A much-valued assistant or "right-hand man." In the novel *Robinson Crusoe* by Daniel Defoe,* Robinson Crusoe was all alone (he thought) on a desert island until the day he met the native who became a most useful companion. Crusoe called him Friday because they met on that day.

man in the gray flannel suit, the   During the 1950's in urban America, many business and professional men wore conservative, gray flannel suits. The fashion provided a colorless, ultraconservative anonymity which masked the personal dramas of the individuals who wore that "uniform." Title of a novel (1955) by American author Sloan Wilson which tells the story of such a man.

man in the iron mask   There actually was a prisoner in Paris' infamous prison, the Bastille, in the time of Louis XIV, who had his face perpetually covered. The mask (of velvet) concealed his identity even from his jailers. Dumas fictionalized this situation in his novel.   —Alexandre Dumas,* *The Viscount of Bragelonne.*

Man never is, but always to be, blest   It is the lot of man to anticipate blessedness but never achieve it in this life.   —Alexander Pope,* *Essay on Man.*

man on a tiger   If one manages to seat himself on a tiger in the first place, he will be safe from the animal's jaws only so long as he does not dismount.   See also: tiger by the tail.

man without a country   The fictional character Philip Nolan, who, having cursed the United States, is sentenced to spend the remainder of his life aboard various ships, never to see his country again or hear any reference made to it.   —Edward Everett Hale, "The Man Without a Country."

Manhattan Transfer   A novel (1925) by John Dos Passos.* The title alludes to a railroad station where passengers change trains, suggesting the way people's paths cross although they live in different worlds and are unknown to one another. The author tells the stories of several such people, presenting a panorama of life in New York City.

manna   Food, or any necessary substance, appearing miraculously from nowhere.   —Bible, Exod. 16:11–15.

man's first disobedience   According to the Book of Genesis, the first time man disobeyed God was when Adam and Eve ate the fruit of the forbidden tree of knowledge in the Garden of Eden.   —John Milton,* *Paradise Lost.*   See also: *Paradise Lost.*

mark of Cain   When God drove Cain away from other men, Cain complained that everyone he might meet would try to kill

him, so God put a mark on him to prevent this.   —Bible, Gen.
4:14–15.   See also: Cain; east of Eden; my brother's keeper.

marry in haste   One who weds in a hurry, goes the saying,
will surely regret it when passions have cooled and he has had a
chance to think about it. The whole expression, "Marry in haste;
repent at leisure," was coined by the American novelist James
Branch Cabell in *Jurgen* (1919).

mea culpa   Latin: "my guilt" or "my fault."   —*The Missal*,
"The Confiteor."

mealy-mouthed   From the Greek *meli-muthos* (honey-
speech) signifying a manner of speaking calculated not to offend;
wishy-washy.

Medusa   In classical mythology, the chief of the Gorgons.
Minerva had turned her hair into snakes and made her face so
horrible that anyone who gazed at her was turned to stone.
Perseus, with the aid of Minerva's shield (which he used as a mirror
so that he would not have to look at Medusa directly), struck off
the Gorgon's head.

meeting of the minds   An agreement or compromise
between two or more persons, perhaps without so much as
resorting to discussion.

Mein Kampf   The title of a book written by Adolf Hitler while
he was in prison after his unsuccessful attempt to overthrow the

German government in 1923. In German, the name means "my struggle." In this book Hitler outlined his racial theories and political and military purposes. Basically, he believed that the German people were racially superior, that the Jews were responsible for Germany's economic woes, and that Germany must conquer foreign territory in order to have the space its people needed if they were to thrive.

melancholy Dane A reference to Shakespeare's Hamlet, a Danish prince, who was very sad over the death of his beloved father and the hasty remarriage of his mother.   —William Shakespeare, *Hamlet*.

men and brethren Thus Peter addresses the 120 or so disciples who gather together in Jerusalem after Jesus is taken up into heaven. Title of a novel (1936) by James Gould Cozzens.   —Bible, Acts 1:16.

mending fences Political expression meaning to go back to one's home community and clean up any unfinished business, especially with the intention of making political friends, attracting more voters, etc.   —Senator John Sherman (1823–1900), speech to his Ohio neighbors.

Mene, Mene, Tekel, Upharsin This is the handwriting that appeared on the wall at Belshazzar's feast. Daniel interprets it as follows: God has finished Belshazzar's kingdom, having found it lacking, and it will be divided between the Medes and the Persians.   —Bible, Dan. 5:1–28.

mens sana in corpore sano   Latin: "A healthy mind in a healthy body."   —Decimus Junius Juvenal,* *Satires.*

Mephistopheles   A devil or evil spirit who first appears in the late medieval Faust legend. He gives Faust renewed youth and knowledge in return for his soul.

Merlin   In the Arthurian legends, a wise old magician who, in return for having engineered the union of King Uther and the Lady Igraine, is given their child, the infant Arthur. He raises Arthur to be a king and assists him from time to time by means of his magic.

message to Garcia   Title of an essay written in 1899, describing the hazardous journey of Lieutenant Andrew Rowan to Garcia, leader of the Cuban rebels. "Carrying a message to Garcia" means undertaking and carrying out a dangerous or important mission with energy and dispatch.   —Elbert Hubbard, *"Message to Garcia."*

Messiah   The Christ; the one chosen to be the leader and deliverer of the Hebrews. The word means "anointed one."

metaphysical conceit   A clever association of things that are basically dissimilar; it is carefully contrived and elaborately worked out. The classic example is John Donne's* detailed comparison of the souls of two lovers with the legs of a pair of compasses in "A Valediction: Forbidding Mourning."

method in his madness   Polonius, observing Hamlet's strange behavior, says, "Though this be madness, yet there is method in't." In other words, there seems to be some sensible, rational thinking taking place underneath the illogical behavior.   —William Shakespeare, *Hamlet,* act 2, sc. 2.

Methuselah   Supposedly the oldest man who ever lived, Methuselah was reputed to have attained the age of 969 years.   —Bible, Gen. 5:27.

Micawber   A man who befriends David Copperfield in the novel of the same name. Mr. Micawber is married, has a number of small children, and is constantly and seriously in debt. He remains calm and cheerful despite this fact, and is always expecting something profitable to "turn up."   —Charles Dickens.*

mice and men   After turning over a field mouse's nest with his plow, the poet observes that "The best laid schemes o' mice and men gang aft a-gley"—that is, often go astray—no matter how carefully the mice or men may plan ahead. The novel *Of Mice and Men* (1937) was written by John Steinbeck.*   —Robert Burns,* "To a Mouse."

Midas   —See: golden touch, the

Middle America   That portion of the U.S. population which tends to abide by traditional conservative values, associated with the middle section of the country, which is relatively insulated from the progressive, cosmopolitan influences which make themselves felt on either coast.

mightier than the sword The pen—or, specifically, the words one writes with it—can, in the long run, make a more lasting impression on the human race than any amount of bloodshed. This phrase was coined by Edward Robert Bulwer-Lytton in *Richelieu* (1839).

miles to go before I sleep The poet, on horseback, pauses between a forest and a lake on "The darkest evening of the year" to contemplate the woods, which are ". . . lovely, dark and deep . . ." Is he, figuratively speaking, on the journey of life? Is the sleep that he will go to, after traveling those many miles, the sleep of death?   —Robert Frost,* "Stopping by Woods on a Snowy Evening."

mills of God The workings of the Almighty. He may seem to move slowly, but he does a thorough job.   —George Herbert,* *Jacula Prudentum.*

Milquetoast A very-meek, henpecked man of middle age depicted in H. T. Webster's famous comic strip, *The Timid Soul.* His given name was Caspar.

mind your p's and q's There are several different versions of the origin of this phrase. The most interesting explanation is that, at one time in England, regular customers of a pub could have a sort of charge account. The pub owner would keep a record of how much they drank and might warn them to mind—i.e., keep track of—their consumption in *pints* and *quarts*.

mind's eye   We make use of the mind's eye when we visualize something, seeing it only mentally rather than through the sense of sight. In the *Symposium,* Plato writes, "Beholding beauty with the eye of the mind he will see not images of it but the reality of it."

Miranda   Heroine of Shakespeare's *The Tempest*. Daughter of Prospero, she is brought up on a desert island with Caliban, the monster, and Ariel, a fairy spirit, as her sole companions. Her name is derived from a Latin word meaning "look" or "wonder," and she is indeed filled with wonder when she beholds the men who are shipwrecked on the island, the only true men she has ever seen besides her father.

Miss Lonelyhearts   A 1933 novel by Nathanael West. The hero is a newspaperman who writes a column of advice to the lovelorn under the pen name "Miss Lonelyhearts."

Mrs. Malaprop   Character in an 18th century play who is best known for her misuse of the English language. Her name comes from the French for "out of place."   —Richard Sheridan, *The Rivals.*

Mistah Kurtz   An African native's rendering of "Mister Kurtz," the white trader living in the African jungle in Joseph Conrad's story. The native has come to report that ". . . he dead." This line is quoted in the prologue to T. S. Eliot's* poem "The Hollow

Men."   —Joseph Conrad,* *Heart of Darkness*.   See also:
(The) horror! The horror!

Mr. Bumble   Minor official of the parish workhouse in which
Oliver Twist, the central figure in Charles Dickens's* novel of the
same name, was born. He was a fat, pompous, hard-hearted man
with an exaggerated sense of his own importance.   See also: The
law is a ass.

Mister Charlie   Hip black slang for any white man, the term
mocks the show of respect formerly demanded by whites
generally.

mixed metaphor   A confused figure of speech in which the
subject is compared with two different things at once. For
example, the metaphors "You've buttered your bread; now you
must eat it" and "You've made your bed; now you must sleep in it"
may become "You've buttered your bread; now you must sleep in
it."

"Modest Proposal, A"   A bitterly satiric essay by Jonathan
Swift,* in which the author proposes solving Ireland's twin
problems of overpopulation and starvation by killing and then
eating the Irish infants.

Modred   The illegitimate son (or nephew, as some versions have
it) of King Arthur. He hates Arthur and helps to bring about the
downfall of the Round Table; in some versions of the story,
Modred mortally wounds Arthur in battle.

money-changers in the Temple   In Jesus' time, it was common for various tradesmen to set up their stands in the immediate vicinity of the house of worship, often within the temple itself. At one point in his ministry Jesus drove these money-changers out of the temple, dramatizing the principle that religion should not be commercialized.   —Bible, Matt. 21:12.

moon is down, the   Shortly before Macbeth murders King Duncan, Banquo asks his son Fleance what time it is, and Fleance replies, "The moon is down; I have not heard the clock." Banquo concludes that it is after midnight. Used as the title of a novel (1942) by John Steinbeck* depicting a conquered people's resistance to the invader.   —William Shakespeare, *Macbeth,* act 2, sc. 1.

Moor, the   Othello, hero of Shakespeare's tragedy of the same name, is often referred to as the Moor or the Moor of Venice. He is a dark-skinned follower of Mohammed, which is true of all Moors, but he is, thanks to Shakespeare's immortal work, always thought of as *the* Moor.

more honored in the breach than the observance
There are two possible interpretations of this quotation. One is: It is a custom which it is more honorable to break than to observe. Another: It is a custom which is more often broken than it is followed.   —William Shakespeare, *Hamlet,* act 1, sc. 4.

more in sorrow than in anger   Prince Hamlet eagerly questions his friend Horatio, who has reported seeing the ghost of

Hamlet's father. Hamlet seems to suspect that the ghost was frowning, for it must be a troubled spirit if it walks about in the night; but Horatio tells him its expression was more sorrowful than angry.   —William Shakespeare, *Hamlet,* act 1, sc. 2.

more sinned against than sinning   More of a victim or injured party than a wrongdoer.   —William Shakespeare, *King Lear,* act 3, sc. 2.

Morgan le Fay   The half-sister of King Arthur; she was gifted with supernatural powers and grew up, in some versions of the epic, to be a real menace to Arthur and his court.

Moses   The Israelites multiplied during their stay in Egypt, and the Egyptians tried to control their population by ordering their male children killed. When Moses was born, his mother hid him as long as she could, then put him in an ark of bulrushes and set it in the river. Pharaoh's daughter found the child and secretly adopted him, knowing him to be a Hebrew. When Moses was grown he saw an Egyptian strike a Hebrew slave, and he killed the Egyptian. Fearing for his life, he fled and became a shepherd.   —Bible, Exod. 1–2.   See also: burning bush.

Most men lead lives of quiet desperation.   Relatively few men suffer extreme, vivid, and conspicuous anxiety such as that experienced by the heroic figures of history or classic tragedy; but most of us, according to the writer, are subject to a persistent despair which is no less harrowing if it is not as epic or spectacular.   —Henry David Thoreau,* *Walden.*

Mount Sinai   —See: Ten Commandments.

Mourning Becomes Electra   Electra was the daughter of Agamemnon (who fought with the Greeks in the Trojan War) and Clytemnestra. She urged her brother to avenge their father's murder by killing their mother and Aegisthus, who was Clytemnestra's lover. *Mourning Becomes Electra* is a trilogy of plays (1931) by Eugene O'Neill* about an American family, the events of which parallel those of the myth. The title means that the expression of grief over her father's death is fitting for her.

moveable feast   A commemorative observance or ceremony which can be celebrated anywhere by those who are initiated. *A Moveable Feast* is a collection of sketches by Ernest Hemingway* of his experiences in Paris in the 1920's.   —Book of Common Prayer (tables and rules).

moving finger writes, the   The author compares life to a story being written by a "moving finger." Once it is written—that is, once an event has happened—there is absolutely nothing that can be done to cancel or change it. Note Robert Graves' translation of this passage—"What we shall be is written, and we are so . . ./By the first day all futures were decided . . ." —suggests that everything we do is foreordained, rather than that the past cannot be altered, as FitzGerald has it. —Edward FitzGerald* (translator), *The Rubáiyát of Omar Khayyám.*

much of a muchness   If two persons or things are much of a muchness, they are practically the same.

mudlark   The antithesis of a skylark, which is associated with soaring, freedom, and brightness. Colloquially a mudlark is a person associated with the gutter, like a street urchin. *The Mudlark* (1949) is a novel by Theodore Bonnet.

mugwump   An Algonquin word for chief. It is used in politics to refer to any party member who votes independently rather than according to party dictates.

multitudes, multitudes   Great numbers of people will face the Lord's wrath on the day of final judgment, says the prophet. God will battle the enemies of Israel "in the valley of decision" and punish them, and Judea will be restored. Title of the book written by one of the characters in Herman Wouk's novel *The Caine Mutiny* (1951).   —Bible, Joel 3:14.

murder in the cathedral   The title of a drama in verse by T. S. Eliot.* The murder in question is that of Archbishop Thomas à Becket in Canterbury Cathedral by the barons of King Henry II.   —See also: Who will free me from this turbulent priest?

murder most foul   So King Hamlet, as a ghost, described his own death at the hands of his brother Claudius.   —William Shakespeare, *Hamlet,* act 1, sc. 5.

Muses   In Greek mythology, these nine daughters of Zeus are the goddesses of the various arts and sciences.

music of the spheres   The ancient astronomer Ptolemy believed that the earth was fixed at the center of a series of transparent, concentric rotating spheres, each carrying one of the heavenly bodies—moon, sun, and the five known planets (the eighth was that of all the stars). The mathematician Pythagoras concluded that the vibrations of the moving spheres must produce different sounds according to their different rates of movement, and that because everything in the universe is observably proportional and orderly, those sounds must be harmonious. The outermost sphere was the *primum mobile* ("first mover") which imparted motion to all the others.

Mutt and Jeff   Two inseparable friends, one tall and the other short. They were the stars of a comic strip created by Bud Fisher in the 1890's.

my brother's keeper   When God asked Cain where his brother Abel was, Cain impertinently replied, ". . . I know not. Am I my brother's keeper?" He meant, of course, that he considered himself responsible only for himself.   —Bible, Gen. 5:9.   See also: Cain; east of Eden; land of Nod; mark of Cain.

my cup runneth over   Whatever one has been given by God or Fate may be compared to a cup containing joy, sorrow, contentment, etc. If one feels that he has been given more than his share of the good things in life, he might say that his cup is full to overflowing.   —Bible, Ps. 23:5.

my druthers   "If I had my druthers" is a homespun way of saying, "If I had my way or preference." The term is a deviation of the phrase "I'd rather," pronouncing it, "I druther."

my Father's business   The young Jesus was telling his parents on earth that he must attend to matters of faith in the service of his spiritual father, God.   —Bible, Luke 2:49.

My God, my God, why hast thou forsaken me? Among the last words spoken by Jesus as he was dying on the Cross. These words are also contained in Psalm 22. Like Jesus' prayer, on the eve of his Crucifixion, that he might be spared, these words reflect his very human antipathy to suffering and death in spite of his sense of mission.   —Bible, Matt. 27:46.

my gorge rises at it   "My stomach turns, I am nauseated at the thought." The gorge is the throat, which contracts involuntarily when one is revolted, as if to vomit. Prince Hamlet is gazing at the fleshless skull of one, long dead, where "hung those lips that I have kissed . . ."   —William Shakespeare, *Hamlet*, act 5, sc. 1.

my heart upon my sleeve   If you wear your heart there, you are displaying it like a badge, telling the world how you feel about someone.   —William Shakespeare, *Othello*, act 1, sc. 1.

my kingdom for a horse!   Shortly before he was killed in battle, King Richard III, in Shakespeare's version, was unhorsed; he went around the battle field crying out for a horse. The horse would have been worth his kingdom, for without it, he knew, he would lose the battle and the kingdom anyway.   —William Shakespeare, *Richard III*, act 5, sc. 4.

my name is Legion   A legion, originally a division of the Roman army, came to stand for any large number of persons. The "man with an unclean spirit" who thus identified himself to Jesus was referring to the supposed fact that he was possessed by many devils.   —Bible, Mark 5:9.

naked came the stranger   Jesus tells his disciples that when he, the Son of man, judges men's souls, he will remember the blessed of the Father who took him in when he was a stranger and clothed him when he was naked, and they will be blessed. Title of a novel (1969) under the pseudonym Penelope Ashe. A hoax, it was actually the work of twenty-odd people, each of whom wrote a chapter independently. The title is not a direct quotation of Matthew, and its resemblance to that passage is apparently coincidental.   —Bible, Matt. 25:35—36.

nation of shopkeepers, a   England, characterized as a nation impelled primarily by the bourgeois commercial motive. Napoleon used the term contemptuously.   —Adam Smith, *The Wealth of Nations* (1776).

(all) nature is but art unknown to thee   All natural or random occurrences, says the poet, are in fact part of a larger pattern and purpose which the individual cannot apprehend; what seems discordant is really harmonious; and "Whatever is, is right."   —Alexander Pope,* *An Essay on Man.*

Nazarene   Jesus, although born in Bethlehem, spent several of his early years, along with his parents, in the village of Nazareth. Therefore, he is sometimes referred to as the Nazarene.

neither snow, nor rain, nor heat, nor gloom of night stays these couriers from the swift completion of their appointed rounds   The inscription on the main post office in New York City is a close paraphrase of Herodotus' description of the ancient Persian messengers.   —Herodotus,* *The Histories.*

never . . . was so much owed by so many to so few   The many are the people of Great Britain—perhaps all the people of the free world; the few are the fighter pilots of the Royal Air Force who, although grievously outnumbered, fought off the attacking German Luftwaffe and won the battle of Britain. —Winston Churchill,* speech in the House of Commons (August 20, 1940).

Never-Never Land   This was the name given to the imaginary land where Peter Pan and his friends lived in Barrie's drama for children. It is supposed to be a place of adventure, excitement, and thrills.   —J. M. Barrie,* *Peter Pan.*   See also: Wonderland.

new broom sweeps clean   A good example of this old proverb would be a new executive or administrator who comes into an organization and makes drastic changes in policies, procedures, and personnel.   —John Heywood,* *Proverbs.*

New Testament   Those books of the Bible which testify to the (new) covenant, or agreement, between God and man which was betokened by the Last Supper.

new wine in old bottles   Jesus says it is not prudent to put new wine in old bottles. By the same token, it would not be fitting for him and his disciples, who represent a new testament, to follow practices prescribed for the old one.   —Bible, Matt. 9:17.

nice Nellie   Someone who is unusually modest, fussy, or prudish in speech, often using euphemisms (words or phrases which are considered tasteful or inoffensive rather than blunt).

Nicodemus   A Pharisee who is at least tentatively receptive to the teachings of Jesus, who shows some support for him before the other Pharisees, and who takes part in the burial of Jesus. —Bible, John 3:1–9; 7:50–51; 19:39.

night has a thousand eyes . . .   —but stars do not light the world as well as the sun. By the same token, despite the myriad ways in which the mind may light one's existence, life's light really dies when love is done, for love is the eye or sun of the heart. The phrase usually suggests merely the sense that one is being watched in the dark.

In 1945, Cornell Hopley-Woolrich published a mystery novel by the name of *The Night Has a Thousand Eyes*.   —*Maides Metamorphosis* (a play attributed to John Lyly).*

nightingale   A European thrush whose singularly melodious nighttime song has inspired poets over the ages. John Keats'* poignant ode is an outstanding example.

Nimrod   A daring, mighty hunter.   —Bible, Gen. 10:8–9.

1984   A novel by George Orwell, published in 1949, which depicts the author's vision of the world twenty-five years later, a projection of the trends he perceived. The central figure lives in a grim, totalitarian society which represses individuality and free thought. The leader, Big Brother, is always watching the citizenry; his name suggests benign, protective paternalism, but in fact he is simply a ruthless dictator whose control of his people is made extremely efficient by the technology he has at his disposal.

Nineveh   Rich and imposing capital of Assyria. One of the nations which beset Israel, Ninevah was founded by Nimrod and destroyed in the 7th century B.C. It is sometimes used as a symbol of luxury, idolatry, and temporal power.

no flies on me   When Christmas nears, the speaker, a mischievous boy called Bill by "the fellers," piously stays out of trouble so he'll get plenty of presents; the rest of the year he is always into something—doesn't sit still long enough for a fly to settle on him.   —Eugene Field,* "Jest 'Fore Christmas."

no love lost If one person loves another who does not love him in return, his love is lost. To say there is no love lost between two people is a dry and subtle way of saying that neither has any use for the other. —Miguel de Cervantes,* *Don Quixote.*

no man is an island That is, no man is isolated from the rest of mankind, whether he thinks he is nor not. Since everyone is part of the "continent" of humanity, each of us is affected by the death of another—just as Europe is diminished when a clod of earth is washed away by the sea. —John Donne,* *Devotions upon Emergent Occasions* (XII).

no man's land An open area lying between the front lines of two conflicting armies. The expression was coined during World War I to describe the disputed area between the trenches of Germany and the Allies.

no room in the inn At the time Jesus was born, his parents, who lived in Nazareth, were in Bethlehem, the city of David, because the Romans required the people to go to their own cities to be taxed. (Jesus' father, Joseph, was ". . . of the house and lineage of David.") The inn in that little town was filled, so when her time came Mary had to deliver the child in a manger among the farm animals. —Bible, Luke 2:7.

Noah's ark Seeing the wickedness of man, generations after Adam, God decided to destroy all men except the righteous Noah and his family. He told Noah to build a huge ark, or boat, and stock it with a male and female ("two and two") of every kind of creature. God then flooded the earth, and only those on the ark survived.   —Bible, Gen. 6–7.

noble savage This term reflects the poet's romantic belief that a man who is untouched by civilization, which tends to corrupt, is naturally honorable and moral.   —John Dryden, *The Conquest of Granada.*

noli me tangere Latin: "Touch me not." Jesus' words to Mary Magdalene when she sees him risen after his Crucifixion and entombment. He tells her this because he is ". . . not yet ascended to [his] Father."   —Bible, John 20:17.

none but the brave deserves the fair The poet's tribute to the conqueror Alexander the Great and his companion at his feast, "the lovely Thais." The poem as a whole is actually a tribute to the power of the music played at the feast, which may be said to conquer the conqueror, overmastering Alexander with its beauty and charm.   —John Dryden, "Alexander's Feast."

none so blind as those that will not see The person who refuses to acknowledge or "see" what is obvious is comparable to someone who actually cannot see at all. —Matthew Henry (1662–1714), *Commentaries.*

Norman Conquest In 1066 William, Duke of Normandy, took an army across the Channel to England and defeated the Saxons, led by King Harold, at the Battle of Hastings. Thus William conquered England and became King, ushering in a new era in English history which culminated in the establishment of the great Plantagenet dynasty one hundred years later.

North by Northwest   There is no such point on the compass. Alfred Hitchcock's classic suspense film of this name, made in the 1950's, takes its title from the line in which Hamlet tells his friends that he is only "mad north-northwest," meaning he merely pretends to be insane.   —William Shakespeare, *Hamlet*, act 2, sc. 2.

not too bright or good for human nature's daily food   The poet extols his loved one as "a phantom of delight," an ethereal, spiritual creature; at the same time, he is gratified to see that she is also quite human, "a woman too," not above having "simple wiles," for example, and capable of ". . . praise, blame, love, kisses, tears, and smiles."   —William Wordsworth,* "She Was a Phantom of Delight."

not with a bang but a whimper   The poet suggests that men, having lost their souls and become passive, colorless, insipid, and empty, are presumptuous to believe that their world will end with a spectacular flourish. Rather, we will go out with a contemptible whimper.   —T. S. Eliot,* "The Hollow Men."

nothing new under the sun   The preacher Ecclesiastes observes that the things which have happened in the past will happen again in the future, and the things that are done now will be done later. No matter how novel an incident may seem, it has surely occurred before in one way or another; the range of human experience is finite.   —Bible, Eccles. 1:9.

nothing will come of nothing   When King Lear abdicates, he tells his three daughters he will divide his kingdom among them, giving the largest share to the one who expresses her love for him most impressively. To his surprise and anger, the youngest, Cordelia, makes a very plain, albeit sincere, statement of her filial affection. When she says she has nothing to add, he observes ominously, "Nothing will come of nothing"—i.e., if she has nothing to say, she will receive nothing in return.   —William Shakespeare, *King Lear,* act 1, sc. 1.

"Nun's Priest's Tale, The"   One of Geoffrey Chaucer's* *Canterbury Tales,* a fictional account in verse of a 14th century pilgrimage to the shrine of St. Thomas à Becket in Canterbury. The author's premise is that each pilgrim tells two stories to entertain the others along the way. This tale is told by the priest who is part of the retinue of a winsome prioress. It is the story of a strutting rooster, Chaunticleer, whose vanity, provoked by the hen Pertelote, almost costs him his life in the jaws of a fox.

O

O death, where is thy sting?   St. Paul writes to the faithful in Corinth that the dead shall be resurrected as Christ was; they who were mortal and perishable shall be made immortal and imperishable. Then Paul exults in this triumph over death, which seems so invulnerable: the sting of death is impotent, and the grave is not victorious.   —Bible, I Cor. 15:55.

O my prophetic soul!   Prince Hamlet does not like his uncle, Claudius, who has—only one month after Hamlet's father's death—married Hamlet's mother and succeeded to the throne. When his father's ghost tells Hamlet that he was murdered by Claudius, this is Hamlet's response. It is as if to say, "I *knew* it!" —William Shakespeare, *Hamlet,* act 1, sc. 5.

O tempora! O mores!   "What times! What manners!"—an expression of incredulous shock or dismay, perhaps good-humored enough, at contemporary behavior which represents a departure from past practices.   —Cicero,* *In Catilinam.*

oaths are straws, men's faiths are wafer-cakes, and hold-fast is the only dog, my duck   Off to the wars in France, an English pub-keeper in William Shakespeare's *Henry V* tells his wife (whom he addresses affectionately as "my duck") not to sell anything on credit; for a promise (to pay) is as perishable as straw, and to take anything on faith is to rely on very flimsy security indeed. The only surety is in holding fast to hard-headed, practical policies like *cash on the barrelhead.*   —*Henry V,* act 2, sc. 3.

Oberon   King of the fairies, husband of Titania. The name can be traced as far back as medieval French legend. At his birth, two gifts were bestowed upon him by the fairies: insight into men's thoughts, and the power to transport himself anywhere in an instant. He is one of the characters in William Shakespeare's *A Midsummer Night's Dream.*

Odysseus   The hero of Homer's* epic poem *The Odyssey.* A victorious veteran of the Trojan War, Odysseus (or Ulysses) has many adventures on his long voyage home to Ithaca.

Oedipus   According to Greek mythology, Oedipus had been separated from his parents in infancy. As a man, he had an altercation with his father, whom he did not recognize, and killed him. Later, ignorant of her identity, he married the widow of the man he had killed—his own mother—and fathered several children by her. When the truth was revealed, his wife-mother killed herself, and Oedipus, in an agony of horror and remorse, blinded himself. "Oedipus complex" is a term coined by Sigmund Freud, the originator of psychoanalysis, to designate the attachment of a child to his/her parent of the opposite sex.

off his feed   When a horse is sick, he does not eat his feed. This expression is often applied to a man who just doesn't quite seem to be himself.

Off with his/her head!   In Wonderland, Alice plays croquet with the Queen of Hearts, a furious woman who repeatedly shouts this command every time someone commits the most trivial offense. (It is never carried out.)   —Lewis Carroll,* *Alice in Wonderland*.

Old Guy, the   In 1605, a Catholic named Guy Fawkes was seized for plotting to blow up England's Protestant King and Parliament. The event is celebrated each November 5th when children go about crying, "A penny for the Old Guy!"—much as American children demand a trick or treat on Hallowe'en. This cry is quoted in the prologue to T. S. Eliot's* poem "The Hollow Men."

"Ol' Man River" A mournful song sung by a black slave, contrasting the shortness and misery of human life as he knows it with the eternal flowing of the Mississippi River.   —Oscar Hammerstein II, "Ol' Man River" (music by Jerome Kern); from the play *Showboat*.

old order changeth, the An established system will inevitably give place to a new one in the course of time. So says King Arthur as he is about to pass away to Avalon in Alfred, Lord Tennyson's* verse version of the Arthurian legend *The Idylls of the King*. Arthur adds that God wills this "lest one good custom should corrupt the world."

Old Testament Those books of the Bible which testify to the covenant, or agreement, between God and Israel, the token of which was the Ten Commandments.

old wives' tale Foolish gossip or a farfetched, perhaps superstitious notion—the sort of thing that might be made up in the kitchen and dispensed over the back fence but which somehow gains general credence. The phrase can be traced back as far as 1220. Arnold Bennett's novel *The Old Wives' Tale* appeared in 1908.

oldest profession prostitution.

olive branch When the earth was flooded after forty days and nights of rain, Noah sent out a dove to see if there was any dry land. The second time he sent out the dove she returned with an olive leaf in her mouth, indicating that the water was going down; thus God had made his peace with mankind. As a sign of his agreement that he would not destroy man again, God set a rainbow in the sky.   —Bible, Gen. 8—9.

Olympus A 9,800-foot peak in Greece, Mt. Olympus was believed to be the home of the immortal gods, led by Zeus.

Onan Son of Judah and grandson of Jacob (Israel). Told by Judah to have intercourse with his brother's widow so that he would provide his brother with an heir, Onan did so, but interrupted the act and "spilled [his seed] on the ground." —Bible, Gen. 38:9.

once more unto the breach A command to charge once more against the enemy. A breach is an opening in the line of defense made by a breakthrough.   —William Shakespeare, *Henry V,* act 3, sc. 1.

one fell swoop One cruel or deadly attack. The allusion is to a bird of prey (falcon, hawk, eagle, etc.) swooping down and making its kill in one fierce stroke.   —William Shakespeare, *Macbeth,* act 4, sc. 3.

one may smile, and smile, and be a villain When Prince Hamlet learns that his uncle Claudius murdered his (the prince's) father, he remembers how cordial Claudius has been and resolves to "set it down" in his memory that one who does evil can smile as much as anyone else. Claudius has taught the prince a lesson in hypocrisy.   —William Shakespeare, *Hamlet*, act 1, sc. 5.

one swallow does not make a summer   The appearance of the first of these birds does not mean that summer has arrived. This principle may be widely applied—e.g., if a man performs one virtuous act, this does not necessarily mean that he is good. —Aristotle,* *Nicomachean Ethics* I.

only thing we have to fear is fear itself, the   In his first inaugural address—in 1933, when the Depression was at its worst—Franklin D. Roosevelt* attempted to instill in the American people a sense of confidence and courage, in the belief that those qualities, in addition to government recovery programs, were necessary if the nation's economy were to recover. Roosevelt was paraphrasing Henry David Thoreau.*

open road   Symbol of the freedom to venture wherever one chooses. Originated by the American poet Walt Whitman,* in "Song of the Open Road" (1856).

Open, Sesame!   In the story "Ali Baba and the Forty Thieves" (in *The Arabian Nights*), the only way to get into a cave full of stolen treasure was to utter the magic words, "Open, Sesame!" (Sesame is a type of herb.) Therefore, any entrance to forbidden or hard-to-get-at places would be an open-sesame.

opportunity knocks but once   The chance to make a decision or commit an act which will change one's life favorably comes to most of us once in a lifetime, if at all. If that chance is allowed to go by—if one does not answer the door at once—it will go away.

The Origin of Species —by Means of Natural Selection.   A book by English naturalist Charles Darwin (1809–1882) setting forth the doctrine of evolution, which states that the great diversity of plants and animals are descended from common ancestors and have developed their differences by responding and adapting to different environments. It is seen as a process which is still continuing. The various species have developed as they have, according to this theory, because their biological structures equipped them to cope with their environments better than other forms, which died out. Thus nature weeded out the latter and "selected" the former to survive.

Orpheus   In Greek myth, a musician who descended into Hades after the death of his wife Eurydice. By means of the wonderful music that he played, he was able to win her release. Unfortunately, he did not observe the condition laid down by the god —that he not look back at her until they had emerged from the underworld—and she was taken back again.

Ossa upon Pelion   Piling trouble onto trouble, difficulty upon difficulty. When the giants of legend attempted to climb up to heaven, they placed Mt. Ossa upon Mt. Pelion in an effort to help them in their ascent. Referred to by Virgil* in his poem "Georgics."

other side of the tracks   In many towns, the railroad line became an arbitrary boundary between the better neighborhoods and those considered inferior. People of either district might use this expression in referring to those across town; the inferior district, of course, might also be disdainfully alluded to as the "wrong" side.

our little life is rounded with a sleep   The enchanter Prospero's beautifully simple characterization of the human experience, suggesting the mystery of what precedes and follows our brief interlude of existence in this world.   —William Shakespeare, *The Tempest,* act 4, sc. 1.

our revels now are ended   The enchanter Prospero creates a charming rustic pageant of spirits for the entertainment of his daughter and her betrothed; then, dissolving the spectacle, he announces that their celebration is concluded.   —William Shakespeare, *The Tempest,* act 4, sc. 1.

our sweetest songs are those that tell of saddest thought   To the poet, the ecstatic caroling of the skylark seems to reflect a higher awareness than mortal men can even dream of, and an utter ignorance of pain. Its joy is pure, not bittersweet, not mixed with sadness, like ours.   —Percy Bysshe Shelley,* "To a Skylark."

Out, damned spot!   Lady Macbeth, who aided her husband in his murder of King Duncan, is troubled by her conscience. In her sleep she tormentedly rubs her hands to remove the spots of blood which it seems to her still taint them.   —William Shakespeare, *Macbeth,* act 5, sc. 1.

out of the mouths of babes   This phrase is used to express the pleased surprise or mild shock of one who hears a child say something precocious.   —Bible, Ps. 8:2.

P

paddle your own canoe   Go your own way; take care of your own affairs; handle the situation in the way that suits you best. The term was first used by the English novelist Frederick Marryat (1792–1848) in *Settlers in Canada*.

pale horse, pale rider   Death is sometimes represented as a horseman seated upon a white or pale horse. Title of a novel (1939) by Katherine Anne Porter.*   —Bible, Rev. 6:8.   See also: four horsemen of the Apocalypse.

Pandarus   An ally of the Trojans. According to the Troilus and Cressida stories, originating in the Middle Ages, Pandarus acted as a procurer for Troilus, arranging his love affair with Cressida.   —See also: Troilus and Cressida.

Pandemonium   The name of Satan's capital in Hell—literally, "the place of all the demons." (According to tradition, Satan led legions of angels in revolt against God, and they were all condemned with him.) The poet describes Pandemonium as a place

of tumultuous uproar.   —John Milton,* *Paradise Lost*.   See
also: *Paradise Lost*.

Pandora's box   In Greek mythology, Pandora was the first
woman. The gods gave her a box containing all kinds of evils,
intended to cause man a great deal of trouble. When the box was
opened, all these evils flew out and began spreading around the
world. However, one gift remained—Hope.

paper tiger   The effigy of a tiger—like those worn in the
celebration of the Chinese New Year—which, despite its fearsome
appearance, is, after all, made only of paper or some other flimsy
material and therefore is not dangerous.

Paradise   The Garden of Eden; heaven; an intermediate place
between earth and heaven.   —Bible, Luke 23:43.   See also:
Cloud-Cuckoo Land; Eden; Shangri-La; Utopia.

Paradise Lost   An epic poem by John Milton.* In the classic
12-book format, Milton tells the story "of Man's first disobedience"
and the expulsion of Adam and Eve from the Garden of Eden.
Milton amplifies the Book of Genesis' account into a detailed and
dramatic rendering of the incident, imaginatively endowing the
principal figures with highly individualized personalities and
exploring their motives minutely. He draws upon the Revelation of
St. John the Divine in order to go behind the events described in
Genesis—e.g., the serpent is shown to be inhabited by Satan—and
give the story cosmic scope. The poet's stated purpose is to "justify
the ways of God to men"—i.e., show man that God was justified in
dealing as he did with Adam and Eve and their descendants.

Parnassus   The highest point of a range of mountains in Greece, supposedly the residing place of Apollo and the Muses.   See also: Apollo, Muses.

Parthian shot   In battle, the ancient Parthians would often turn their horses around and appear to be retreating. Then, with their enemies off their guard, they would, while still moving away, let fly with one final fusillade of arrows. Figuratively, getting in a last insulting or witty remark while in the act of leaving (or seeming to leave) would be a Parthian shot.

parting of the Red Sea   When Moses brought the Israelites to the Red Sea (actually the Reed Sea, a much less formidable body of water) on their flight from Egypt, God parted the water so they could cross. The pursuing Egyptians followed, and the water rushed back, destroying them.   —Bible, Exod. 14:21–31.   See also: pillar of cloud and fire; Ten Commandments.

passing strange   Surpassingly, exceedingly strange and therefore remarkable—characterizing the awed and wondering attitude of Desdemona as she listens to Othello's recital of his travels and exploits.   —William Shakespeare, *Othello*, act 1, sc. 3.

Passover   Pharaoh refused to free the Israelites from bondage in Egypt despite a succession of plagues God visited upon the country; consequently, God moved across the land destroying the firstborn in every Egyptian house, but passing over the houses of the Israelites, which were marked by the blood of ritually slaughtered lambs. Thus began the Exodus.   —Bible, Exod. 12.

pathetic fallacy   Attributing human qualities like sorrow or happiness to inanimate things—as in the phrase "the cruel sea"—shows, in the opinion of the English writer and critic Ruskin, a sad and pitiable lack of good sense.   —John Ruskin, *Modern Painters.*

paths of glory   The progress of mighty and famous men. The poet says that such men move, just as unimportant people do, "to the grave;" in the end they are no better than anybody else. Title of a novel (1935) by Humphrey Cobb.   —Thomas Gray,* *Elegy Written in a Country Churchyard.*   See also: the great leveler.

patience of Job   —See: Job.

Patience on a monument   A statuary figure representing the quality of patience; therefore, used to refer to someone who shows no outward signs of sorrow, longing, grief, etc.   —William Shakespeare, *Twelfth Night,* act 2, sc. 4.

Pavlov's dog   Ivan Pavlov (1849–1936), a Russian physiologist who discovered conditioned reflexes, found that a dog could be trained to salivate whenever it heard a bell or saw a circle of light because it had come to associate those stimuli with food.

Pax Romana   Latin: "Roman peace," referring to the peace existing among the different peoples of the Roman Empire, who might have been at each other's throats if the Romans had not conquered them. Perhaps peace is cheap at any price; still, a *Pax Romana* has overtones of imposition.

pay for a dead horse   If one contracts to buy a horse, and the animal dies after he takes possession of it but before the price is paid, then—unless there is a warranty provision to the contrary—he must still come across with the money. Of course it is demoralizing to have to pay for something of which one no longer has the use.

peace in our time   British Prime Minister Neville Chamberlain, returning from the 1938 Munich Conference (where England and France handed over most of Czechoslovakia to Hitler in an ill-advised attempt to avoid a war), announced, "I believe it is peace for [not "in"] our time." He was wrong, of course. —Book of Common Prayer.

pearl of great price   Usually a symbol of something precious and truly valuable. In a parable, Jesus compares the kingdom of heaven to such a pearl, and the anonymous Pearl Poet of the 14th century uses the gem similarly. However, in his 1947 novel *The Pearl*, John Steinbeck* tells of a pearl which brings its discoverer misery and misfortune.

pearls before swine   Jesus warns his followers not to throw pearls under the feet of pigs—that is, not to waste anything valuable upon those who cannot or will not appreciate it. The term is frequently used to discourage the waste of wisdom on the ignorant.   —Bible, Matt. 7:6.

Peeping Tom —See: Lady Godiva.

penal colony A remote enclave to which convicted felons are shipped from the mother country for long-term imprisonment and hard labor, usually under very difficult and unpleasant conditions. "In the Penal Colony" is a story by the Bohemian writer Franz Kafka (1883–1924).

Penelope and the shroud Odysseus' wife Penelope was virtually a widow for nineteen years while her husband fought in the Trojan War and wandered abroad afterwards. During that time many men sought her hand in marriage, and she told them she would make her decision when the shroud she was weaving for her father-in-law was finished. It never was, for each night she would undo the portion she had woven that day.

perchance to dream In his misery, Prince Hamlet contemplates suicide, feeling that it would be a blessed relief "To die: to sleep . . ." Then a disturbing thought occurs to him: In "that sleep of death," perchance, one may "dream"—that is, enter a dream-like afterlife in which he will be punished for the crime of suicide.   —William Shakespeare, *Hamlet*, act 3, sc. 1.

Percival The holiest of King Arthur's knights of the Round Table. In some versions of the Arthurian legends, he is the only one who was privileged to see the Holy Grail.

Peter Jesus' leading Apostle, one of the first Jesus enlisted, and one of his favorites; the one to whom Jesus gave ". . . the keys of the kingdom of heaven." Originally a fisherman named Simon, he was called by Jesus and renamed "Cephas," meaning "rock" (which was rendered as "Peter" in Greek) because of the strength and firmness of character Jesus saw in him. It was on this rock, Jesus said, that he would build his church.   —Bible, John 1:40—42; Matt. 16:18.

Peter Pan   A boy who never grew up; the hero of a play of the same name who lives in Never-Never Land with his companion Tinkerbell and a company of lost boys. He has many adventures with pirates, Indians, etc.   —J. M. Barrie,* *Peter Pan.*

Peter's pence   Voluntary offerings made by Roman Catholics to the Holy See of Rome. Originally, it was an annual tribute of one penny, collected from every family, paid at the feast of St. Peter.

Petrified Forest, the   The word *petrified* literally means "turned to stone," and the Petrified Forest of Arizona is just that—the fallen trunks of trees aeons old whose wood fibers were gradually replaced by sedimentary particles of stone while they were submerged in a primordial sea long since receded. The trunks still have the appearance of wood with grain and bark. This is the title of a play (1935) by the American dramatist Robert E. Sherwood.

Pharisees   —See: generation of vipers.

Philistines   Pagan inhabitants of Palestine with whom the Israelites often came into conflict after they fled Egypt. The word *philistine* has come to mean someone who is insensitive, materialistic or crude, and ignorant of finer things. See also: David; Delilah; Samson.

phoenix A fabulous bird appearing in the mythologies of several ancient civilizations. Near the end of its life, the phoenix burns itself to ashes, and from these ashes arises the reborn phoenix.

phony war, the Designating the period in World War II (late 1939 and early 1940) after Germany conquered Poland and before she overran France. Virtually no fighting took place during this time.

physician, heal thyself Before attempting to heal others, a physician should heal himself. This is a proverb quoted by Jesus in the synagogue of his own city of Nazareth. He says the Nazarenes will surely tell him this—i.e., to work wonders in Nazareth as he is reported to have done in Capernaum, to cure at home if he cures abroad; but, says, Jesus, "No prophet is accepted in his own country."   —Bible, Luke 4:23.

Pickwickian sense In Dickens's* comic novel, a member of the very ceremonious Pickwick Club contemptuously refers to Mr. Pickwick himself with a shockingly opprobrious term, saying, "The honorable gentleman was a humbug." When asked if he had used the term in a common sense, the gentleman would not withdraw his statement, and replied that he had, rather, used it "in its Pickwickian sense," adding that he had the highest esteem for Mr. Pickwick. Mr. Pickwick's outraged dignity and honor were at once assuaged. Thus this term applies to uncomplimentary words which do not have the same force that they usually have.   —Charles Dickens, *The Pickwick Papers*.

piece of work, a   "What a piece of work is a man!" marvels Prince Hamlet. How excellent a creature God has made him! —William Shakespeare, *Hamlet,* act 2, sc. 2.

Pied Piper of Hamelin   A fellow dressed in parti-colored clothing who was able to play his flute in such a way as to make rats or people follow him spellbound.   —German folktale.   See also: you must pay the piper.

Piers Plowman   Central figure in a 14th century allegorical poem, Piers is a hard-working, unassuming farmer who advocates industry and piety as the means of gaining access to Truth. —William Langland, "The Vision of Piers Plowman."

Pilgrim's Progress, The   A pilgrim is one who travels to a holy place to demonstrate his piety, and it may be said that the life of every pious man is a pilgrimage to heaven. *The Pilgrim's Progress* is an allegorical narration of an ordinary man's pilgrimage from the City of Destruction to the Heavenly Gates. On the way, the pilgrim, Christian, passes through such places as the Slough of Despond and the Valley of Humiliation and meets such persons as Hopeful, Lord Hategood, and the Giant Despair.   —John Bunyan.

pillar of cloud and fire   God led Moses and the Israelites out of slavery in Egypt and to their new home, taking the shape of a cloudy column by day and a fiery one by night.   —Bible, Exod. 13:21.

pit and the pendulum Two of the fiendish tortures devised for the narrator of Edgar Allan Poe's* short story of the same name, who was taken prisoner by the Spanish Inquisition.

place in the sun, a As plants reach out for the sunlight they must have in order to grow, so men long to have the opportunity to escape the shadow of confinement so that they may thrive and enjoy the fruits of their labor. Title of a full-length movie based on Theodore Dreiser's* novel *An American Tragedy* (1925).   —Bernard von Bulow, speech before the Reichstag (1897).

plague on both your houses, a Modern interpretation: "To hell with both of you!" A way of expressing one's lack of sympathy with either side in a dispute.   —William Shakespeare, *Romeo and Juliet*, act 3, sc. 1.

Platonic love Love on a very elevated plane—ideal rather than sensual; spiritual rather than romantic; a meeting of minds. The philosopher Plato extolled the mind and condemned bodily appetites.

play cat and mouse Cats have the reputation of toying (sadistically, it appears to us) with the mice they prey on instead of dispatching them quickly.

play in Peoria   Originally a show business expression. If a show, movie, or act of any kind will play in Peoria (Illinois), it will be acceptable to most average people—to those who have come to be referred to as "Middle America."

play it again, Sam   Line never spoken by Humphrey Bogart (or anyone else) in the 1942 film *Casablanca*. Bogart said, "Play it!" Ingrid Bergman said, "Play it, Sam." The expression, nonetheless, has come, in a way, to stand for Bogart. American film director, writer, and actor Woody Allen wrote a play (later a film) with the same title, about a young man who identifies himself with the Bogart image.

play it as it lays   The way a (presumably ungrammatical) golfer is supposed to play any shot after his tee shot, unless the rules permit him to improve his lie—i.e., he must try to hit it no matter how awkwardly it may be positioned. Generally, the phrase means to take things as they come and make the best of them.

play within a play   A play, or part of one, presented within the framework of another play. The most famous example occurs in *Hamlet,* in which the actors put on a performance of *The Murder of Gonzago* before the royal audience consisting of Hamlet, the King and Queen, and the rest of the court.   —William Shakespeare, *Hamlet,* act 3, sc. 2.

play's the thing, the   Prince Hamlet hopes that when the actors put on their dramatization of a murder, the guilty king, watching the play, will in some way betray his guilt—that in

the play Hamlet will "catch the conscience of the king."
—William Shakespeare, *Hamlet,* act 2, sc. 2.

playwright   A playwright *writes* dramatic dialogue, but in a
larger sense he *makes* or *builds* a three-dimensional, operating
mechanism with moving parts, as it were, which is called a *play.*
Thus he is a craftsman, in essentially the same way as a shipwright,
say, who builds ships.

Please, sir, I want some more.   Desperate, a hungry little
boy politely asks for an additional portion of the miserable gruel
served to the undernourished children in the workhouse. His
request is considered presumptuous, and the boy suffers the
outraged displeasure of the master, the beadle and the
board.   —Charles Dickens,* *Oliver Twist.*

pleasure bent   "Bent" in the sense of "inclined" or
"directed." To be pleasure bent is to be seeking pleasure.

plowed with my heifer   To obtain information by unfair
means, such as a disloyal friend, is to plow with another's heifer
(cow). This happened to Samson twice. On one occasion the
Philistines extorted information from his wife; later they bribed the
harlot Delilah to discover his secret.   —Bible, Judg. 14:18.

poetic justice   A reward or punishment which is so fitting and
appropriate that it seems the stuff of poetry rather than reality.
The phrase was first used in Alexander Pope's* satirical poem *The
Dunciad.*

poetic license   The authority to use language in unconventional, imaginative ways for artistic effect. There is no bureau to apply to, and no certificate is issued; whenever one sits down to compose a poem, he automatically has poetic license.

point of no return   The midpoint in a journey for which a fixed amount of fuel is available. Once past this point, one must go ahead; since more than half the fuel is exhausted, there is no possibility of going back. Title of a novel (1949) by the American author John P. Marquand.

poor fool   King Lear, turned out into the storm by his elder daughters, to whom he has given up his kingdom, bewails his miserable condition and belatedly pities his fool (jester), who suffers with him. Later, he mourns his one faithful daughter, Cordelia, referring to her as his poor fool—perhaps in this case it is a quirky term of endearment; perhaps he associates her fidelity with that of his jester, or feels that by unjustly accusing her earlier he trifled with her affection; or perhaps the boy actor who played the fool was playing the part of Cordelia in this last scene of the play!   —William Shakespeare, *King Lear*, act 3, sc. 2; act 5, sc. 3.

Poor Richard   The fictitious author of *Poor Richard's Almanac*, which was actually written by the young Benjamin Franklin.*

Poor Tom o' Bedlam   A madman. In Shakespeare's *King Lear*, Edgar, son of the Duke of Gloucester, assumes the identity of Poor Tom to avoid being killed.

posh   Elegant, luxurious, first-class; referring to hotels, transportation, furnishings, etc. Often supposed to stand for Port Outward, Starboard Home (meaning that the best accommodations on British steamships were on the port side when leaving England and on the starboard when coming in, because considering the times of departure and arrival, this would afford one more sunlight). There seems to be no firm evidence to support this etymology, however.

pot-boiler   A piece of hack writing or inferior art of some other form which is torn off simply to bring in some money and keep one's pot of food boiling.

potter's field   A burial ground intended for poor, criminal, or unknown persons. The original one was located near Jerusalem, and is thought to have been the field of a potter at one time. The priests bought it with the money paid Judas to betray Jesus. Judas had returned the money in an agony of remorse, and the priest could not keep "blood money" in the Temple.   —Bible, Matt. 27:7.

pound of flesh   Shylock, a moneylender, demanded that a man who was unable to pay back a certain amount of money should be compelled to give him a pound of flesh from his body as agreed. Demanding a pound of flesh means insisting on what one feels is due to him, even if it is unreasonable to expect it.   —William Shakespeare, *The Merchant of Venice.*

power and the glory   Phrase from the conclusion of the

Lord's Prayer according to the King James Version of the Bible.   —Bible, Matt. 6:13.

practice to deceive   To lie or conceal the truth, which often makes it necessary to continue the practice. In the romantic narrative poem *Marmion*, Sir Walter Scott* says that one who does this weaves "a tangled web" of falsehoods in which, presumably, he will sooner or later be caught.

Pre-Raphaelite Brotherhood   A group of 19th century painters who were dissatisfied with the formal, classical style which prevailed in their time and turned to medieval forms and subjects for their inspiration. They thought of the Italian painter Raphael (1483–1520) as the turning point between the romantic Middle Ages and the Renaissance.

preserve, protect, and defend   In taking his oath of office, the President of the United States swears to "preserve, protect, and defend the Constitution." *Preserve and Protect* (1968), by American author Allen Drury, is a novel about Washington politics.

Priapus   In Greek mythology, the god of fertility and reproductive power. In later times he was considered the chief god of obscenity and lust.

pride goeth before a fall   A person who is too proud of his accomplishments will surely end up taking a (figurative) fall. —Bible, Prov. 16:18.

primal curse   The very first (primal) crime, according to the Book of Genesis, was Cain's killing of his brother Abel. God, discovering the murder, put a curse upon Cain.   —William Shakespeare, *Hamlet,* act 3, sc. 3.

primrose path of dalliance   The sensuously beautiful and romantic avenue along which one indulges illicit, fleshly impulses.   —William Shakespeare, *Hamlet,* act 1, sc. 3.

primum mobile   —See: music of the spheres.

Prince Hal   The young Henry, heir to the English throne, who became King Henry V. As a prince he led a rollicking, irresponsible life with his companion Sir John Falstaff.   —William Shakespeare, *King Henry IV,* Parts I and II; *King Henry V.*

Prince of Darkness   One of many names for the Devil. He is also referred to as Satan, Lucifer, Old Nick, Scratch, etc.

princess and the pea, the   According to the fairy tale, only a true princess of royal blood should be sensitive enough to feel one pea placed beneath several layers of mattresses. —Hans Christian Andersen.*

Procrustean bed   In greek mythology, Procrustes was a robber from Attica who would capture unwary travellers and force them to lie upon his bed. If they were too short, he would stretch them until they fit; if too long, he would chop off the excess length.

Therefore, forcing people's actions or thoughts to fit a predetermined mold is putting them into the Procrustean bed.

prodigal son   Jesus tells of a young man who left his father to go to the big city, where he wasted all his money. He returned home to find that his father, instead of disowning him, greeted him joyfully and treated him as well as his brother, who had stayed home and been thrifty.   —Bible, Luke 15:11–32.   See also: eleventh hour, at the; kill the fatted calf.

Prometheus   "Forethinker." In Greek mythology, one of the Titans. He created men out of mud and water and then, feeling sorry for them, stole fire from heaven and gave it to them. For this offense, Zeus had him chained to a mountain top, where an eagle preyed on his liver all day, the liver being renewed at night. He was finally freed by Hercules, who killed the eagle. *Prometheus Bound,* a 5th century B.C. Greek tragedy by Aeschylus, depicts the Titan in chains; *Prometheus Unbound,* a verse drama by Percy Bysshe Shelley,* depicts his release.

Promised Land   A place or condition of complete satisfaction, in which one has everything he has hoped for. God promised Abraham, Issac, and Jacob that he would give their descendants "a land flowing with milk and honey."   —Bible, Exod. 33:1–3.

promises like pie crust   Those that are easily broken.

prophet without honor in his own country   This was

Jesus' experience when he returned to his own part of the country after preaching to multitudes of people in other towns. The people in his own synagogue were not impressed. "Is not this the carpenter's son?" they said.   —Bible, Matt. 13:53–58.

Prospero   Deposed as Duke of Milan by his scheming brother, Prospero——the central figure in Shakespeare's *The Tempest*——was set adrift with his infant daughter in a dilapidated boat which carried them to an uncharted island. A friend had secretly provided him with the books he loved, however, and by diligent study of the "liberal arts" he became an enchanter and——as his name suggests——prospered.   —Act 1, sc. 2.

proud man's contumely   When contemplating suicide, Hamlet reviewed some of the worst "ills that flesh is heir to." Among these he listed "the insolence of office," "the law's delay," and the scornful, insulting manner of the proud man.
—William Shakespeare, *Hamlet,* act 3, sc. 1.

Providence   Since God provides for those who serve him, he is sometimes referred to as Providence.   See also: Isaac; lilies of the field.

publicans and sinners   In the Roman Empire, publicans were wealthy businessmen involved in managing State monopolies and overseeing the collecting of taxes. They became very unpopular with the common people, and in Jesus' time they were often regarded as no better than sinners and often mentioned in the same breath.   —Bible, Matt. 11:19.

Puck A young spirit, full of mischief and fun, used as a messenger by Oberon, King of the fairies in Shakespeare's *A Midsummer Night's Dream*. Also called Robin Goodfellow.

pull in one's horns To hold back; to take back an expressed opinion; to keep one's strong feelings to oneself. The figure of speech refers to the snail, which retracts the hornlike protuberances with which it probes its surroundings and goes back into its shell when startled.

pull out all stops To let go completely; to give all one has; to attack a situation with all one's energy. The expression very likely can be traced to the playing of large pipe organs; the pulling out of all the stop knobs would create a good deal of sound.

pumpkin eater According to the nursery rhyme, Peter the pumpkin eater "had a wife and couldn't keep her"—at least not until he ". . . put her in a pumpkin shell." *The Pumpkin Eater* is a novel (1962) by Penelope Mortimer.

punishment fits the crime In a comic operetta, the clever and bloodthirsty emperor of Japan (Mikado) sings a song about inventing various penalties to be inflicted on evildoers: "My object all sublime/I shall achieve in time/To let the punishment fit the crime."   —Gilbert* and Sullivan, *The Mikado*.

purple passage An unusually spectacular passage of a literary work—e.g., a speech in a play—which does not blend naturally with the rest, perhaps because the ideas it contains or the mode in which they are expressed is out of character. In any case, the passage is like a splash of lurid color on the text.

put the cart before the horse   One ought to deal with the elements of a problem in logical order, first things first—i.e., the horse, naturally, ought to go before the cart it is supposed to pull.   —John Heywood,* *Proverbs.*

Put out the light, and then—Put out the light!   Preparing to kill his wife, who he believes has been unfaithful, Othello reflects on the finality of his act: if he snuffs out a candle, it can be lit again; but he will not be able to rekindle the light of Desdemona's life once he has extinguished it.   —William Shakespeare, *Othello,* act 5, sc. 2.

Pygmalion   According to the Greek legend, Pygmalion was a sculptor who created the statue of a beautiful young woman, Galatea. He fell in love with the statue, which was magically brought to life. Title of a play (1913), by George Bernard Shaw,* depicting a phonetics teacher's transformation of the guttersnipe Eliza Doolittle into a fine lady. This play was the basis of the musical comedy *My Fair Lady* (1956), by Alan Jay Lerner and Frederick Loewe.

Pyrrhic victory   A victory won at too heavy a price. After his victory over the Romans at Asculum (279 B.C.), which cost the lives of his best officers and men, King Pyrrhus of Epirus declared, "One more such victory and we are lost."

Q

quarrel in a straw Disgusted by his failure to take decisive action against his uncle the King, who he knows murdered his father, Prince Hamlet observes that "when honor's at the stake," one ought to fight at the slightest provocation, let alone when one's father has been murdered. ——William Shakespeare, *Hamlet*, act 4, sc. 4.

Quasimodo A deaf, hunchbacked bell-ringer who falls in love with the gypsy girl Esmeralda in Victor Hugo's novel of medieval France. The name is formed from Latin words of the introit of the Mass for the Sunday after Easter: *quasi modo geniti infantes* (as newborn babes). In fact, Quasimodo *is* very childlike. ——Victor Hugo, *The Hunchback of Notre Dame* (1831).

Queeg, Captain Philip Francis In Herman Wouk's novel *The Caine Mutiny* (1951), master of a U.S. destroyer-mine-sweeper in the Pacific in World War II. Queeg is a disturbed man who drives his crew wild by his obsession with petty details of discipline, and is relieved of command by his executive officer at the height of a typhoon. One of the Freudian clues to his paranoia is his habit, when under stress, of rolling two steel ball bearings in his hand.

Queen of Sheba   A fabulously wealthy monarch who came to Jerusalem to see if all she had heard of Solomon's wisdom and riches were true. She was duly impressed and gave him many expensive gifts in acknowledgment.   —Bible, I Kings 10.   See also: Solomon.

Quixotic   Don Quixote, hero of Miguel de Cervantes'* novel of the same name, is foolishly brave and ridiculously gallant. He fights losing battles in worthless causes and idealizes a woman of light and easy virtue as a knight would put his lady on a pedestal.   See also: tilting at windmills.

R

race is not to the swift, the   Not always or necessarily, at any rate; nor do the strong always win battles, nor the wise become rich, nor men of skill gain favor. Everyone is subject to "time and chance," the accidents of circumstance.   —Bible, Eccles. 9:11.

Rachel weeping for her children   Rachel was the long barren wife of Jacob, patriarch of Israel. The children she is said to have wept for were the innocents slaughtered by King Herod at the time of Jesus' birth, when Rachel was long dead. Thus the grief which the matriarch would have felt for her descendants symbolizes the grief of the nation. (The same phrase was used in the same way to suggest the sorrow that would attend the subjection of the Jews by Babylonia in the time of Jeremiah.)   —Bible, Matt. 2:18; Jer. 31:15.

rag and a bone and a hank of hair, a The poet's definition of a woman who is indifferent to the pleas of the man who worships her.   —Rudyard Kipling,* "The Vampire."

rage, rage against the dying of the light The poet urges his dying father not to surrender his life passively, but to struggle passionately to the end.   —Dylan Thomas,* "Do Not Go Gentle into that Good Night." See also: into that good night.

rage to live, a An intense passion for life which, says the poet, will kill the one who feels it. Title of a novel (1949) by John O'Hara.   —Alexander Pope,* *Moral Essays.*

rainbow —See: olive branch.

raising Cain —See: Cain.

Rake's Progress, The A rake (what we would call today a playboy) is depicted in a series of brutally realistic etchings by the 18th century English artist William Hogarth. In each picture of the series, the rake has slipped lower and lower in life, until at the end he is old, sick, and insane. In the 20th century, Igor Stravinsky wrote an opera with the same title.

ram in the thicket —See: Isaac.

Rape of the Lock, The Alexander Pope's* poem satirizing fashionable 18th century society. It tells, in epic style—as if the silly incident were world-shaking and as heroic as the Trojan War—how a young man snips a lock of a lady's hair.

Rapunzel In the old fairy tale, Rapunzel was a beautiful girl with very long hair. She was locked up in a tower, but she let her long hair hang down, and her lover was able to climb up it to reach her.

Rashomon An old Japanese tale of rape and murder. Told from several different points of view, it points up the difficulty of determining the objective truth of any human event. In the 20th century it was made into a very successful film by Kurosawa.

Raskolnikov A poor Russian student in Feodor Dostoevski's* novel *Crime and Punishment* (1866), he murders an old woman (a pawnbroker) and her sister. His conscience will not permit him to accept his own attempts to justify the act, and he finally confesses to Petrovich, the shrewd detective who has been stalking him.

Rasputin A compelling Russian holy man of the early 20th century who, miraculously, it seemed, stopped the bleeding of the Tsar's son, a hemophiliac. The boy's parents, overcredulous in their gratitude to this hypnotic monk, made him their favorite, and he came to exert a great deal of political power through the Tsar in spite of his well-known bouts of drunkenness and sprees of womanizing. When a Russian prince attempted to assassinate him, to save Russia from his demonic influence, he discovered to his horror that cyanide was not sufficient; Rasputin had to be shot repeatedly and finally drowned.

raveled sleave of care   Macbeth compares the cares and tribulations that accumulate about us to a vexing tangle of thread which, he says, sleep enables us to "knit" into a more orderly and manageable form.   —William Shakespeare, *Macbeth*, act 2, sc. 2.

raven   A bird which often foreshadows evil or unhappy events, including death. Edgar Allan Poe* wrote a famous poem called "The Raven."

read between the lines   To understand the intent of a writer or speaker, even though that intent may not be present in so many words.

readiness is all   Prince Hamlet observes fatalistically that death may come now, or it may come later; "yet it will come." The time is unimportant; the only thing that matters is that one should be prepared to meet it.   —William Shakespeare, *Hamlet*, act 5, sc. 2.

reap the whirlwind   —See: sow the wind.

reason not the need   Do not make bare necessity the test in determining what one should be allowed to possess; for if one is permitted to own no more than he needs to survive, "Man's life is cheap as beast's."   —William Shakespeare, *King Lear*, act 2, sc. 4.

Red Cross Knight   Symbol of holiness in Edmund Spenser's* *The Faeire Queene* (Book I).

red herring   That which confuses or clouds an issue by figuratively setting a false trail. In fox hunting, dragging a red (smoked) herring across the fox's trail will cause the hounds to lose the scent. English detective novelist Dorothy Sayers wrote *The Five Red Herrings* in 1931.

red letter   A red letter day is one on which something special or out of the ordinary takes place. Calendars often print weekends and holidays in red ink, with the weekdays in black.

red tape   A tape of that color was once used to tie up bundles of official government documents. That tape has become synonymous with the confusion and delay which are often met when one who is dealing with a bureaucracy is forced to follow a prescribed official routine—filling out forms in triplicate, waiting to have a document stamped or initialed—which results in a great deal of paperwork, largely unnecessary.

Renaissance   Literally, rebirth—the emergence into the mainstream of European society of the learning and culture which were the heritage of ancient Greece and Rome after the Dark Ages of ignorance and violence; roughly, the 14th to 17th centuries. This period was marked by a flowering of the arts and the beginnings of modern science, and characterized by a humanistic interest in the Classical period.

rend one's garments   In ancient times it was customary to ritually tear one's clothing slightly on occasions of extreme grief, remorse, or shock. When the high priest asked Jesus if he was the Son of God and Jesus replied, "Thou hast said," the priest, horrified at what he considered blasphemy, rent his robes. —Bible, Matt. 26:63–65.

render unto Caesar   Give to worldly rulers the respect due to them, and to God the worship due to him.   —Bible, Matt. 22:21.

rendezvous with destiny   An appointment with Fate. The speaker was President Franklin D. Roosevelt,* in 1936, telling his fellow Americans that they must prepare to meet the great challenge of their time.

rest is silence, the   The last words uttered by Hamlet before he dies.   —William Shakespeare, *Hamlet*, act 5, sc. 2.

Richard III   King of England, 1483–1485. In Shakespeare's play, Richard is portrayed as hunchbacked and mentally and physically deformed, a man who murders several of his relatives in order to reach the throne. It is widely thought today that this picture of the monarch is inaccurate.

riddle of the sphinx —See: sphinx.

riddle wrapped in a mystery inside an enigma A semi-humorous Western definition of Russia. The author of this saying (Winston Churchill,* in 1939) was possibly thinking of a Chinese puzzle, consisting of several boxes nested one inside the other.

riding for a fall Almost asking for trouble by thoughtless or heedless actions or words, as a reckless horseman risks being thrown.

Rima The "bird-girl" heroine, who understands the language of nature, of English author W. H. Hudson's 1904 novel, *Green Mansions.*

Rip Van Winkle In the early days of New York, when it was still a Dutch colony, there lived a young man, so the story goes, named Rip Van Winkle. He fell asleep one day and slept for twenty years. Needless to say, when he awoke, he found that many changes had taken place.   —Washington Irving, "Rip Van Winkle."

ripeness is all A man must submit to death, just as he does to birth; he has nothing to say about the circumstances of either. The only thing for one to be concerned about is that he be "ripe"—i.e., ready—when death comes.   —William Shakespeare, *King Lear,* act 5, sc. 2.

ritzy   Very high-class, expensive, elegant. From the Ritz-Carlton hotel in New York City, which in turn was named after its founder César Ritz.

river of time   —See: time is a river.

road not taken   The poet recalls how he stood at a fork in the road of his life, wondering which way to follow—the one well traveled, or the one which "was grassy and wanted wear." He chose the latter; the path most people travel is the road not taken by the poet.   —Robert Frost,* "The Road Not Taken."

road to Damascus   Saul, an enemy of Jesus' followers, was converted to Christianity when Jesus appeared to him in a vision while he was on his way to Damascus. He later changed his name to Paul, and became one of Jesus' most devoted apostles. —Bible, Acts 9:3–20.

road to hell is paved with good intentions   The earliest traceable source of this expression makes no mention of a road; it simply implies that hell has many inhabitants who "meant well" but never got around to doing it.   —George Herbert,* *Jacula Prudentum* (a book of proverbs).

rob Peter to pay Paul   The story goes that, during the reign of England's Edward VI, the lands of St. Peter at Westminster were taken over by the king—in order to raise money needed to repair St. Paul's Cathedral in London.   —John Heywood,* *Proverbs.*

Robespierre   Maximilien François Robespierre (1758–1794), a leader in the French Revolution. The so-called Reign of Terror was largely his responsibility; it ended only when he himself was sent to the guillotine.

Robin Goodfellow   —See: Puck.

Roman holiday   A wild, reckless celebration; an orgy of carefree abandon or violence. The original reference was to the death of a gladiator in the arena ("Butchered to make a Roman holiday"); it appeared in Lord Byron's* romantic narrative poem *Childe Harold's Pilgrimage.*

romance   A work of literature dealing with far-off times and places, mystery, legend, heroic adventure or affairs of the heart; it is the antithesis of realism or naturalism, and is frequently associated with the age of chivalry. A romantic person tends to be idealistic, to look at the world through rose-colored glasses, and to be a dreamer.

root of all evil   Not money, but the *love* of money. —Bible, I Tim. 6:10.

rose between two thorns   An attractive and/or delicate person situated between two persons who are unattractive or rough and abrasive.

rose-colored glasses   To look at the world through such glasses is to see it suffused with a beautiful glow—everything looks "rosy"; one sees it not as it is, but as one would wish it to be.

Rosencrantz and Guildenstern   Two courtiers, old friends of Prince Hamlet's, who are used by the King to spy on Hamlet. They are completely willing to be employed as spies, presumably because of the preferment that they might gain. In the end they are caught up in the treachery to which they lend themselves and are killed.   —William Shakespeare, *Hamlet.*

Rosetta Stone   A stone found in Egypt in 1799 by a French officer of engineers. The discovery of this stone made it possible for the Egyptologist Champollion to decipher the ancient Egyptian hieroglyphics. The expression may be used to designate the key to a difficult problem.

rosy-fingered dawn   An expression often used by the author to describe a beautiful sunrise.   —Homer,* *The Iliad.*

round table   So that no one of King Arthur's knights would feel that he was higher or lower than any of his fellows, a round table was used for their councils.

royal we   It has always been the custom, in nearly all countries, for reigning monarchs to refer to themselves in the plural, at least in public. For instance, Queen Victoria's comment, "We are not amused," meant simply that *she* did not find anything humorous in what was being done. This mark of distinction may stem from the concept of "divine right," the belief that a monarch reigned by the will and sponsorship of God. The plural pronoun could mean "God and I."

Rube Goldberg device   A fantastically complex convenience "machine" designed to perform some ridiculously simple task, such as pour a cup of coffee. Some of the "parts" of the machine are docilely co-operative persons and animals whose responses to certain stimuli trigger later movements in the chain that culminates in the desired function. Rube Goldberg was a cartoonist who became famous for a whole host of such "inventions."

rumors of wars   The unpleasant noises of battle. Jesus was telling his followers that before the end of the world, there would be more wars and destruction. *A Rumor of War* (1977) is a book of personal narratives about the Vietnam war by Philip Caputo.   —Bible, Matt. 24:6.

Rumpelstiltskin   Funny-looking, dwarfish little man who, in return for spinning straw into gold to save a Princess' life, demands that she give him her first-born child. He agrees to give her one chance to keep the baby: she must discover what the little man's name is. She does find out, just in time.   —German folktale.

run the gauntlet   An ordeal. The gauntlet (more accurately, gantlet) consists of two rows of men who face each other armed with clubs, sticks, or the like. As a test or punishment, another man is forced to run the length of the rows and be struck by these weapons as he goes.

S

sackcloth and ashes   In biblical times, it was the Hebrew custom for someone to wear sackcloth (a coarse, dark cloth) and ashes as an expression of mourning, penitence, etc.   —Bible, Esther 4:1; Dan. 9:3.

Sadducees   —See: generation of vipers.

St. Agnes   Patron saint of young virgins. At the age of thirteen, she was sentenced to be burned at the stake, but the fire went out, and Aspasias drew his sword and cut her head off. John Keats* wrote a poem called "The Eve of St. Agnes."

St. Joan   Joan of Arc, known as the Maid of Orleans. While still a mere girl, she claimed to hear heavenly voices directing her to lead the army and drive the English out of France. She did assume military leadership, raise the siege of Orleans in 1429, and bring about the crowning of Charles VII. However, soon after that, she was taken prisoner by the English and burned as a witch and heretic. In 1920 she was proclaimed a saint by the Catholic church. She appears in many works of literature, among them Mark Twain's *Personal Recollections of Joan of Arc* (1896), Anatole France's *Life of Joan of Arc* (1908), and George Bernard Shaw's* play *Saint Joan* (1923).

Salome   —See: dance of the seven veils.

salt of the earth   Since salt is a preservative—virtually the only one available in ancient times—it is associated with permanence. To refer to someone as the salt of the earth is to say that he enjoys the particular blessing of permanence—as far as the people of Israel were concerned, the permanence of their special relationship with God, for example. Because of the great value of salt in ancient times, as a commodity and as a medium of exchange, the expression also implies excellence.   —Bible, Matt. 5:13.   See also: worth one's salt.

Samson   One of the "judges" (leaders) of Israel after the death of Joshua. A man of great strength, he fought the Philistines, original inhabitants of Palestine. He once killed 1,000 Philistines with the jawbone of an ass.   —Bible, Judg. 14.   See also: Delilah; eyeless in Gaza; Philistines.

Samson Agonistes   A sacred drama by John Milton,* based upon the biblical story of Samson and Delilah. The title means, in Greek, Samson's Struggles.   See also: Delilah.

Sancho Panza   The rotund, materialistic, and comic squire of Don Quixote, in Miguel de Cervantes'* novel of the same name, who rides behind his master on a donkey and complements the angular Don's sober idealism. Sancho is admirably loyal and steadfast, however, and experiences great sadness at Don Quixote's final disillusionment.

Satan   The Devil.   —Bible, Job 1:6.   See also: Lucifer;
Serpent.

Saturday's children   According to the rhyme, the child who
is born on a Saturday "has to work for its living." Title of a play
(1927) by Maxwell Anderson.

Savoyard   An admirer of, or performer in, the works of
Gilbert and Sullivan, whose comic operas were for many years
performed at London's Savoy Theatre. William S. Gilbert*
(1836–1911) and Arthur S. Sullivan (1842–1900) were the
author and composer of some of the most popular light musical
works of the English-speaking stage, including *H.M.S. Pinafore*,
The Pirates of Penzance, and *The Mikado*.

saying Peace, peace; when there is no peace   The
prophet, speaking for God, says that the priests and prophets of
Jerusalem "have healed . . . the hurt . . . of my people slightly"
—that is, given them false comfort. These men, who ought to set a
pious example, have become greedy; they have figuratively given
themselves to the false gods which stand for self-serving.
—Bible, Jer. 6:14.

scales fall from the eyes   The moment when truth or
understanding dawns upon a person is compared to the miraculous
healing of the sight of a blind person.   —Bible, Acts 9:18.

scapegoat   One made to bear the blame for the wrongdoing
of others. Part of the ancient Hebrew ritual for the Day of

Atonement was as follows: Two goats were brought to the altar of the tabernacle; one was sacrificed to the Lord. The high priest then, by confession, transferred his sins and those of his people to the other goat, which was then led to the wilderness and allowed to escape. Title of a novel (1957) by Daphne du Maurier.

scarlet letter, the   In Puritan New England during the 17th century, a scarlet "A" (for adulteress) was sewn on the dress, or in some cases branded on the flesh, of any woman caught in adultery. Nathaniel Hawthorne* wrote a novel (1850) called *The Scarlet Letter,* recounting the story of Hester Prynne's illicit affair with the young minister, Arthur Dimmesdale.

scarlet woman   A prostitute; a woman with a bad reputation. Scarlet has long been a color associated with sinfulness. —Bible, Rev. 17:4.

Scheherazade   —See: *Thousand and One Nights, The.*

screw your courage to the sticking place   Attempting to steel her husband's nerve, Lady Macbeth tells him to wind himself up tightly and determinedly and aim at the target. If he does, she says, they will not fail in their attempt to murder the king. —William Shakespeare, *Macbeth,* act 1, sc. 7.

scribes   —See: generation of vipers.

Scylla and Charybdis   One of the dangers faced by

Odysseus (Ulysses) and his crew was to navigate their ship through the treacherous waters flanked by the twin monsters, Scylla and Charybdis. Thus these names have come to stand for two equally dangerous threats through which one must pass as through a gauntlet.   —Homer,* *The Odyssey*.

sea change   A complete and utter change, such as takes place in a human body which has lain at the bottom of the sea for a long period.   —William Shakespeare, *The Tempest*, act 1, sc. 2.

Second Coming, the   As seen in the dream-vision of St. John the Divine, Christ returns to earth, first as a lamb, then as a fearsome figure with a sword coming out of his mouth, mounted on a white horse. He is met in battle by the dragon Satan, accompanied by the kings of the earth and their armies, whom he defeats. All are killed but Satan, who is cast into hell for a thousand years. Title of a poem by William Butler Yeats.*   —Bible, Rev. 14:1–5; 19:11–21; 20:1–2.

see eye to eye   To look at things in exactly the same way as another person; to agree completely in all details with someone else.   —Bible, Isa. 52:8.

seek, and ye shall find   Jesus tells his followers that the way to obtain the truth is to look for it actively; he says that all who look sincerely will indeed find the truth.   —Bible, Matt. 7:7–8.

sell one's birthright   Isaac, son of Abraham and his wife Rebekah, had twin sons. Esau was born moments before Jacob, so he had the right to inherit from their father. One day, when Esau was dying of starvation, Jacob refused to feed him unless he swore to give up his birthright, and Esau did so. Later, when Isaac was dying, Jacob impersonated Esau, and Isaac made him lord over his brothers. An angel changed his name to Israel, and his ten sons and two grandsons became fathers of the twelve tribes of Israel.   —Bible, Gen. 25:21–34; 27; 32:24–32.   See also: coat of many colors; . . . knew not Joseph.

separate peace, a   If two nations are at war with a third, one of the former might break off hostilities, leaving the war to continue one against one. Similarly, an individual soldier might, if he is put out of action by a wound or decides to desert, for example, make his own "separate peace" with the enemy. No treaty is signed in this case, of course—the soldier simply withdraws. Title of a novel (1959) by John Knowles.   —Ernest Hemingway,* *In Our Time—A Very Special Short Story.*

separate the wheat from the chaff   Chaff is the waste portion or husk of the grain which is separated from the kernel in threshing. Figuratively, any things or persons may be threshed or sifted in order to set aside those which are useful, good, or true and dispose of the rest. John the Baptist, for example, says that Jesus will "gather his wheat [righteous men] into the garner; but he will burn up the chaff [sinners] with . . . fire."   —Bible, Matt. 3:12.

sermons in stones   Nature is a great teacher, and the poet believes that trees, brooks, stones, etc., all have something to teach the observant man.   —William Shakespeare, *As You Like It,* act 2, sc. 1.

serpent   The snake in the Garden of Eden which maliciously tempted Eve to eat the fruit (it is *not* identified as an apple) of the tree of knowledge, which God had forbidden them to touch under pain of death. She then gave the fruit to Adam. According to St. John the Divine, Satan was in the serpent (dragon).   —Bible, Gen. 3:1–6; Rev. 12:7–17.   See also: Adam; Eden; Eve; fig leaves; Satan; tree of knowledge.

serving two masters   Trying to obey two opposite, conflicting codes of behavior.   —Bible, Matt. 6:24.

set a thief   —See: to catch a thief.

set the teeth on edge   The taste (real or figurative) of something bitter or unpleasant would cause one to make a wry face and perhaps feel as if one's teeth were tingling with discomfort.   —Bible, Ezek. 18:2; Jer. 31:29.

set the world on fire   To create a sensation; to commit deeds which cause some large change to take place in the world.

Setebos   The god worshipped by the witch Sycorax, mother of Caliban in William Shakespeare's *The Tempest.* In Robert Browning's* poem "Caliban upon Setebos" (1864), Caliban speculates on the power of that deity.

seven ages of man, the   The speaker says that all men go through seven periods of their lives: the infant, the school-boy, the lover, the soldier, the justice, the old man, and the person in his second childhood or senility.   —William Shakespeare, *As You Like It*, act 2, sc. 7.

seven deadly sins   The seven "deadly" or worst sins are pride, lust, avarice, anger, envy, gluttony, and sloth.

Seven Wonders of the Ancient World   The pyramids of Egypt; the hanging gardens of Semiramis at Babylon; the statue of Zeus at Olympia; the temple of Diana at Ephesus; the mausoleum at Halicarnassus; the Colossus at Rhodes; the seventh wonder has been variously identified as the Pharos of Egypt, the walls of Babylon, and the palace of Cyrus.

Seven-Year Itch, The   Title of a play by George Axelrod. Supposedly, after seven years of marriage, the average husband finds himself restless and looking for romantic adventure.

seventh seal, the   In his dream-vision, St. John the Divine is taken, in spirit, up into heaven where he sees God on a throne. In his hand God holds a book sealed with seven seals. Only the Lamb (Christ) is able to open them. As the first four seals are opened, the four horsemen of the Apocalypse emerge. The opening of the fifth reveals the souls of those slain for their faith in God, and that of the sixth a cataclysmic upheaval. When the seventh is opened, seven angels sound their trumpets, the seventh signalling Christ's assumption of dominion over the earth and, ultimately, his triumph over Satan, the millennium, and the last judgment.   —Bible, Rev. 4—8.

Shadrach, Meshach and Abednego The Babylonian names of three captive Israelites who, with Daniel, were groomed to serve King Nebuchadnezzar. When they refused to worship the King's gods, he had them thrown into a fiery furnace, but their faith in God saved them from harm. —Bible, Dan. 3. See also: Belshazzar's feast; by the rivers of Babylon; Daniel in the lions' den.

shake the dust off your feet Get out of there as fast as you can. Move on to another location, with no regretful looking back. —Bible, Matt. 10:14.

Shangri-La A fictitious land where all is peaceful and no one grows old, as depicted in James Hilton's novel, *Lost Horizon*. —See also: Cloud-Cuckoo Land; Eden; Paradise; Utopia.

shape of things to come H. G. Wells used this expression as the title of a novel depicting the world as it might evolve many years in the future. —William Shakespeare, *Troilus and Cressida.*

Shibboleth A password or secret saying, known only to the chosen ones. It can also mean an old, worn-out belief. Its literal meaning is "a stream in flood." In a war between Gilead and Ephraim, the Gileadites required those who passed through their lines to say this word. The Ephraimites pronounced it improperly "Sibboleth." Thus they were easily identified and slain. —Bible, Judg. 12:1—6.

Ship of Fools An allegorical satire written by Sebastian Brant in 1494. The ship in the story was manned by various types of fools; by this means, the author attacked the vices and weaknesses of his day. There have been several re-workings of the same theme, among them the novel *Ship of Fools* (1962) by Katherine Anne Porter.*

ships that pass in the night   In its original context this is a metaphor for the many brief, tenuous encounters with others that each of us has in life—distant, fleeting, mere passing acquaintance-ships that are never to be renewed: "Only a look and a voice; then darkness . . ."   —Henry Wadsworth Longfellow,* *Tales of a Wayside Inn.*

shoes of the fisherman   The apostle Peter, originally a fisherman, was, according to Roman Catholic doctrine, made the first Pope by Jesus himself. Anyone figuratively wearing the shoes of the fisherman would, therefore, be Pope. Title of a novel (1963) by Morris L. West.

showing the white feather   Acting in a cowardly manner. The phrase comes from cockfighting, in which a white feather in the tail of the gamecock supposedly shows that it comes of inferior stock.

shuffle off this mortal coil   At death, one thrusts aside or shrugs off the miseries of his mortal existence as a butterfly divests itself of its chrysalis.   —William Shakespeare, *Hamlet,* act 3, sc. 1.

Shylock   A hard-hearted moneylender or usurer (one who lends money at excessively high interest).   —William Shakespeare, *The Merchant of Venice*.   See also: pound of flesh.

Sibyl   A female prophet or fortune-teller. In the ancient legends of various civilizations, sibyls were women who, with divine guidance, made predictions.

Sic transit gloria mundi.   Latin: "So passes away the glory of the world." This phrase, expressing the temporary nature of everything human, is quoted during the coronation ceremony of the Pope. It originates in the treatise *De Imitatione Christi,* by the German ecclesiastic Thomas à Kempis (1380—1471).

signs of the times   Incidents, situations, or attitudes which symptomize or characterize an era. Jesus berates the hypocritical Pharisees and Sadducees, who can "discern the face of the sky" but cannot discern the truth he speaks.   —Bible, Matt. 16:3.

Silent, upon a peak in Darien   The author has just read a translation of the works of Homer, author of the *Iliad* and the *Odyssey*. He feels like a man who has discovered a new land, comparing himself to Balboa's men (the poet mistakenly refers to Cortez) standing in awe on a hill in Darien (Panama) as they view the Pacific Ocean for the first time.   —John Keats,* "On First Looking into Chapman's Homer."

Simon Legree   The cruel Yankee overseer of the Negroes on the St. Clare plantation, a despicable villain who whips the good slave Uncle Tom to death in Harriet Beecher Stowe's* novel *Uncle Tom's Cabin.*

Sing no sad songs for me   The 19th century English poet means, "Do not mourn for me when I am dead."   —Christina Rossetti, "Song."

sinister   The Latin word for "left." Traditionally, the left side is associated with evil, ill fortune or trouble, probably simply because left-handed people are a minority. This association was reinforced by such biblical dicta as "A wise man's heart is at his right hand; but a fool's heart is at his left" (Eccles. 10:2) and numerous references to "the right hand of God" as a place of favor (e.g., Mark 16:19). It has been perpetuated in many ways, including the superstitious practice of tossing spilled salt over the left shoulder—in the direction of the devil which lingers there. (This practice was probably suggested by the fact that Judas, the Apostle who betrayed Christ, was once depicted as having upset a container of salt at the Last Supper.)

sins of the fathers   The Old Testament belief that children should, and would, be punished by God for the evil deeds committed by their parents.   —Bible, Exod. 20:5; Euripides, *Phrixus.*

Sisyphus   A legendary king of Corinth who, after his death, was given the task of rolling a large stone up a hill. The stone kept rolling back down, making his task a never-ending one.

sixes and sevens   In a state of confusion; unable to reach an agreement. The expression comes from gambling with dice. —William Shakespeare, *Richard II,* act 2, sc. 2; Miguel de Cervantes,* *Don Quixote.*

skeleton in the closet, a   Supposedly, every family has at least one hidden, shameful secret it wishes concealed from the world.   —William Makepeace Thackeray,* *The Newcomes.*

skin of one's teeth, the   Escaping from death or danger in this manner is escaping by a hair's breadth, just barely getting away. *The Skin of Our Teeth* is a play (1942) by the American dramatist Thornton Wilder.   —Bible, Job 19:20.

slaughter of the innocents   Numerous times in the Bible, large numbers of innocent men, women, and children were massacred, either by conquerors, rulers, etc., or by God himself. In his desire to crush any potential threat to his power, Pharaoh ordered the death of many infants. Later, God slew all the first-born children in Egypt. Probably the most famous incident of this kind occurred when Herod ordered the extermination of all young children in his attempt to destroy the newborn Jesus.   —Bible, Exod. 1:15–22; 12:29; Matt. 2:16.

sleep no more   Macbeth, guilt-ridden because of his murder of King Duncan, imagines he hears a voice crying, "Sleep no more! Macbeth does murder sleep!" The king had been stabbed as he lay in bed asleep in Macbeth's home.   —William Shakespeare, *Macbeth*, act 2, sc. 2.

slough of Despond   A deep, nearly impassable bog through which Christian, the hero of John Bunyan's allegorical tale *The Pilgrim's Progress* (1678–1684), must pass. Figuratively, a fit of deep depression.

smoke-filled room A room or area which is the site of political wheeling-and-dealing. The term was first employed as part of a prediction by Senator Warren G. Harding's manager that the 1920 Republican National Convention would be deadlocked, and that a group of men sitting "around a table in a smoke-filled room" would decide the outcome. He was correct: Harding was nominated in just such circumstances.   —Harry M. Daugherty.

smoking pistol/gun, the If someone is shot, and you see a man holding a pistol which has obviously just been fired, the chances are that he did the shooting. Thus the smoking pistol is the evidence that establishes an obvious link between an act and the person who committed it. A term frequently invoked in the course of the Watergate scandal of the early 1970's.

soapbox orator Someone who gets up on a platform (originally a soapbox or similar small object) to make a political speech to a small crowd in a park or similar public place.

Socratic irony Pretending to be ignorant and asking questions in a way which is calculated to lead one's opponent into a point. This definition is somewhat misleading; for although, according to Plato, Socrates frequently used this method, he also repeatedly and sincerely acknowledged that he was not positive that he knew all the answers. He invited anyone who could do so to prove that he was wrong, saying he would be grateful for such help in arriving at the truth.

Sodom and Gomorrah Two cities which were destroyed,

because of their wickedness and immorality, by fire and brimstone from heaven.   —Bible, Gen. 19:1—25.   See also: Lot's wife.

Solomon   Son of Israel's King David and Bathsheba; noted for his wisdom and the glory of his reign, which culminated in his erection of the Temple, built of timbers cut from the cedars of Lebanon. Later, his foreign wives turned him away from God, and God said that after his death the kingdom would be divided, which it was.   —Bible, I Kings 2—11.   See also: Queen of Sheba; Song of Solomon; wisdom of Solomon.

Some animals are more equal than others.   In a fable, animals revolt against their master and take over the farm. They then set up a number of commandments, one of which is "All animals are equal." One day, however, it is seen that the animals who are in charge of the new communist-like society have added the clause ". . . but some animals are more equal than others." This absurd statement shows that those who are in power in such a society tend to try to enjoy privileges while still claiming that no one is entitled to have more than anyone else.   —George Orwell, *Animal Farm.*

some mute inglorious Milton   The poet is considering the possibility that, among those buried in the little village cemetery, there might lie the remains of someone who had the potential to be a great poet, but nevertheless died unknown or unhonored. —Thomas Gray,* "Elegy in a Country Churchyard."

something will turn up   —See: Mr. Micawber.

Son of Man, the   So Jesus often referred to himself.

Song of Solomon   One of the books of the biblical Old Testament. Although it reads like a love poem, it is often interpreted as an allegory of the union between Christ and his Church.

sorcerer's apprentice   A very old tale of a young assistant to a wise old magician who tries to imitate some of his master's tricks. He only succeeds in getting into trouble when the brooms he has trained to carry water cannot be halted; the return of the sorcerer to the scene saves the day. Walt Disney's film *Fantasia* contains a segment featuring Mickey Mouse as the young apprentice, with music by Paul Dukas.

sound and fury   A good deal of noise with no real meaning to it, such as might be made by a madman. Macbeth says that life is "a tale/told by an idiot, full of sound and fury,/signifying nothing." In 1929, the American novelist William Faulkner* wrote a novel called *The Sound and the Fury*.   —William Shakespeare, *Macbeth*.

sour grapes   In the fable, a fox was unable to reach high enough to pluck some grapes, so he declared that they must be sour. In other words, if one cannot attain what he is after, he speaks slightingly of it, as if he hadn't really wanted it all along.   —Aesop,* *Fables*.

sow wild oats   To live recklessly, for pleasure only; often used with a sexual connotation. The point seems to be that it is only natural for the young to act irresponsibly, but that age will have a calming or reforming influence. The term originated in Samuel Butler's novel *The Way of All Flesh* (1903).

sow the wind . . . and reap the whirlwind. To bring about serious consequences because of one's reckless or heedless actions.   —Bible, Hos. 8:7.

spare the rod A parent who never uses physical punishment is only going to spoil the child.   —Bible, Prov. 13:24.

sparrow's fall, the God takes such an interest in the welfare of even his most humble creations that he notices the fall of a little bird.   —Bible, Matt. 10:29.

Speak for yourself, John. Among the 17th century Puritan settlers of New England was the middle-aged soldier Miles Standish. According to Henry Wadsworth Longfellow's* narrative poem *The Courtship of Miles Standish,* he sent his young friend John Alden to court the maiden Priscilla on Miles' behalf, but she replied, "Why don't you speak for yourself, John?" She and Alden were eventually married.

Speak of the Devil . . . and his horns will appear. It often happens that, just as we are talking about someone, he will come along.   —Samuel Taylor Coleridge,* *Biographia Literaria* (a book of essays on literary criticism).

Speak softly and carry a big stick. Talk or behave in a calm manner, but be able to back up your words or deeds with muscle, if the need arises.   —Theodore Roosevelt, speech at the Minnesota State Fair (September 2, 1901).

speaking in tongues The ability claimed by some mystics and religious groups (specifically Pentecostal) to converse in and understand unknown languages.   —Bible, Acts 2:4.

sphinx A monster of ancient Greek and Egyptian mythology. The riddle of the Grecian sphinx (represented as a winged lion with a woman's head) was solved by Oedipus. The riddle was: "What goes on four feet, on two feet, and three, but the more feet it goes on the weaker it be?" The answer: Man, who as an infant goes on hands and knees, in maturity on two legs, and in old age uses a staff or cane as a third leg. The Egyptian sphinx (represented as a wingless lion with the head and breast of a man) was a symbol of royal power or the sun god. The colossal sphinx at Gizeh, near the Great Pyramid, was carved out of limestone about 2620 B.C.

spirit is willing, the . . . but the flesh is weak. That is, one's better, nobler instincts dictate one's manner of behavior, but human or fleshly desires make it difficult to carry out these instincts.   —Bible, Matt. 26:41.

spit and image or spitting image To say that one man is the spit and image of another is to say he is the exact likeness of the other fellow, "right down to the very spit in his mouth." "Spitting image" is probably a corruption of the first term.

In Genesis 2 and 3 it is said that God made man "in his own image" and "breathed into his nostrils the breath of life." This earthy image of man's creation, with its suggestion of the intimate interchange of breath, may have inspired the expression.

splendor in the grass   The poet has grown away in time from God, his glorious origin, and "nothing can bring back the hour of splendor in the grass, of glory in the flower"—the sense of unmixed joy he felt when he was a boy. American playwright William Inge wrote the screenplay for the 1961 film *Splendor in the Grass*.   —William Wordsworth,* "Ode: Intimations of Immortality."

SPQR   Abbreviation for the Latin phrase, *Senatus Populusque Romanus* ("the Roman Senate and People"), which was inscribed on the standards of ancient Rome.

Stand a little out of my sun(light)   Comment made by the old philosopher Diogenes to conqueror Alexander the Great, who had asked if there was anything he could do for Diogenes. —Plutarch,* *Lives.*

stand on ceremony   This frequently means to prefer or to insist on following formal, ceremonial procedures in any social dealings. Originally it meant to take stock in or be influenced by religious ceremonies which are conducted for the purpose of forecasting the future. When the priests' rituals resulted in an unfavorable omen for Julius Caesar, he refused to stand on this ceremony and went to the Senate in spite of the omen. —William Shakespeare, *Julius Caesar*, act 2, sc. 2.

star-cross'd lovers   The young Romeo Montague and Juliet Capulet; so-called because it seemed that their stars (that is, their astrological signs) doomed them to a brief, unhappy life together.   —William Shakespeare, *Romeo and Juliet* (prologue).

stately pleasure-dome   The poet's description of the magnificent palace of the Oriental ruler, Kubla Khan.   —Samuel Taylor Coleridge,*-"Kubla Khan."

steal a march   If you march your army before the other general moves his, you may be able to seize the advantage.

steal someone's thunder   To undercut an advantage a person might have had by using it before he can or by simply exposing it prematurely. John Dennis (1657–1734), a dramatist who devised a thunder sound effect for his own play, which was unsuccessful, found that his technique was being used in other plays that were well received.

stiffnecked people, a   An epithet frequently applied to the Israelites in the Old Testament, reflecting God's exasperation with their pride and stubbornness and their propensity to backslide or turn away from him to the worship of pagan gods.   —Bible, Exod. 32:9.

still small voice   This phrase usually means one's conscience, which quietly but persistently tells one what he should or should not do. In its original context it was the voice of God speaking to the prophet Elijah. On Mt. Horeb, Elijah, having fled from the evil Jezebel, witnessed a wind, an earthquake, and a fire, but God was not in them. It was then that he heard the still small voice.   —Bible, I Kings 19:12.

still waters run deep   The quiet, unassuming person must have (so the saying implies) some great hidden emotions. As Quintus Curtius (1st century A.D.) put it, "The deepest rivers flow with the least sound."

Stoic   Originally, a follower of Zeno, who founded the school of Greek philosophers called Stoicism about 308 B.C. He gave lectures on a public colonnade or porch called *Stoa pokile,* hence the name. They believed that virtue was the highest good and that the passions and appetites should be kept firmly in check. The term is often applied to one who shows little or no outward signs of emotion.

straight and narrow   The road to goodness. Actually, Jesus said, "Strait [meaning narrow] is the gate, and narrow is the way, which leadeth unto life, and few there be that find it."   —Bible, Matt. 7:14.

strain at a gnat and swallow a camel   To be extremely finicky about small details, but overlook more important matters. —Bible, Matt. 23:24.

strange bedfellows   To further their own political aspirations, men of widely differing political philosophies sometimes find themselves working side by side. The phrase was first used by the American editor, essayist, and novelist Charles Dudley Warner (1829–1900) in his book of essays, *My Summer in a Garden.*

straw dogs   Effigies of dogs, fashioned from straw, were used for sacrifices. Afterwards they were simply cast away.   —Lao Tzu, *The Way of Lao Tzu.*

straw man   An imaginary or fictitious person whose existence is stated or supposed for some purpose.

straw that broke the camel's back   Something small or trifling which, added to previous small or trifling things, proves to be too much.   —Charles Dickens,* *Dombey and Son.*

straws in the wind   Seemingly trivial incidents may foreshadow the coming of important events. Included in *Table Talk,* the book of sayings of the English jurist and scholar John Selden, which was compiled by his secretary after Selden's death.

stream of consciousness   A term, originally used in early 20th century theories of psychology, employed as a literary technique in which character and events are revealed through the thought processes of one of the characters in the story. The device has been used by such well-known authors as Poe,* Melville,* Virginia Woolf, Hemingway,* and O'Neill.*   —William James, *The Principles of Psychology.*

strike while the iron is hot   Do it now! Act while you have the opportunity. The best time for a blacksmith to hammer out a piece of metal was when the material was red-hot.   —Publilius Syrus, *Maxims.*

Sturm und Drang   The name given to the intellectual awakening of Germany in the late 18th century. Some of Germany's greatest poets and dramatists were associated with this literary movement; its basic characteristic was the extravagant passion of the literary characters. The German expression means "storm and stress." The name of the movement is taken from the play *Sturm und Drang* by Frederick Maximilian von Klinger.

Styx In classical mythology, the river that flowed around the regions of Hades. After death, spirits would be taken across this river by the ferryman Charon to the other world.   —See also: Achilles.

substance of things hoped for, the evidence of things not seen St. Paul's definition of faith.   —Bible, Heb. 11:1.

such stuff as dreams are made on The enchanter Prospero observes that all of us are as insubstantial and dream-like as the figures in the vision he has just created and dissolved.   —William Shakespeare, *The Tempest,* act 4, sc. 1.

suffer fools gladly To put up with one's mental inferiors patiently.   —Bible, II Cor. 11:19.

suffer the little children . . . Jesus was telling his followers to allow (suffer) the young people in the crowd to approach him; their simple faith was what was needed to enter the Kingdom of Heaven.   —Bible, Mark 10:14.

sugar-coated pill An unpleasant truth delivered in a relatively pleasant way.

sun also rises, the   Ecclesiastes, the preacher, speaks of the uselessness of human effort. He refers to the never-ending cycle of the sun to show how brief each man's life is by comparison. Title of a novel by Ernest Hemingway* depicting the experience of an expatriate American in France and Spain in the years following World War I. It was published in 1926.   —Bible, Eccles. 1:5.   See also: "Ol' Man River".

Sun King   King Louis XIV of France, who ruled from 1643 to 1715. His reign was notable for his patronage of literature and the arts.

survival of the fittest   According to the theory of evolution, those organic forms best fitted to cope with their environments and compete for food and mates will survive; less successful forms must die out. If this principle is applied to society, it would appear to dictate that people who are ill-fitted to compete for economic gain—e.g., because of intellectual inferiority or reticence or some other supposed deficiency—must become extinct. Such an application of his theory is not implicit in Darwin's work.   —Herbert Spencer, *Principles of Biology.*

Svengali   The name of the sinister Hungarian musician who controls the singing of Trilby O'Ferrall in George du Maurier's novel *Trilby.* A Svengali is one who holds a strange or hypnotic power over another.   See also: Trilby.

swan song   The final work by a poet, artist, composer, etc. According to legend, the swan sings a beautiful song just before dying.   See also: after many a summer dies the swan.

Sweeney Agonistes   A satirical figure created by T. S. Eliot,* Sweeney is a symbol of the materialistic, brutal, and sensual man of the 20th century. He appears in several poems, in addition to the play *Sweeney Agonistes,* the title of which is a pun on Milton's* *Samson Agonistes.*   See also: Samson Agonistes.

sweetness and light   "The two noblest things." Lately, the expression has often been given a touch of sarcasm or cynicism, as if it referred to blind optimism. Coined in Jonathan Swift's* satirical *The Battle of the Books* (1704).

sweets to the sweet   So saying, Prince Hamlet's mother sadly scatters flowers upon the coffin of the innocent maiden who, she adds, she hoped would have been her son's wife. —William Shakespeare, *Hamlet,* act 5, sc. 1.

sword of Damocles   An ever-present threat to one's life or well-being. Dionysius the Elder, ruler of ancient Syracuse, dramatized the constant threats to a king's life by having Damocles sit in a chair over which was a sword suspended by one single hair.

sword in the stone, the   Arthur, as a boy, was the only person in the land who was able to pull a sword out of a stone. This deed proved that he was in fact the rightful ruler of Britain; he then became King Arthur. It is thought that the sorcerer Merlin was responsible for placing the sword in the stone. Title of a modern treatment (1939) of the Arthurian legend by T. H. White.

T

take the bull by the horns   To confront a difficulty boldly, as one might seize the horns of a threatening bull and contend with it instead of running away from it.

take the fifth   To call upon the Fifth Amendment to the U.S. Constitution, which states that one accused of a crime shall not be forced to testify against himself. Thus, if a person feels he might be incriminated by his answer to a question, he may refuse to answer.

take the will for the deed   To be satisfied with another's intention to do something even though, for some presumably good reason, he never did it. The term originates in Rabelais's satirical *Gargantua and Pantagruel* (1532–1564).

take with a grain of salt   To be skeptical; to have reservations about the reliability of a person or idea. Presumably, a bit of salt added to a dose of bad-tasting medicine will make it easier to swallow. Attributed to Pompey in the *Natural History* of Pliny the Elder (23–79 A.D.).

talents   In a parable, Jesus tells of a man who entrusts several

servants with talents (money) while he is away, expecting them to invest the money profitably. The servant who returns his talent unused is cast out. The man represents God, and the talent, any kind of ability; so the parable means that God expects one to use whatever ability he has, no matter how small. It is because of this parable that the word "talent" came to mean "aptitude."
—Bible, Matt. 25:14—30.

talking head The effigy of a human head from which a voice—simulated, artificially reproduced, or conveyed from a distance—is made to issue. According to tradition, there were a number of these in ancient and medieval times, some of which could also be made to move. Modern technology has made it possible to create very lifelike talking-moving heads. The term is sometimes applied to the image of a television personality, such as a newsman or commentator, who usually appears on the screen as if he were a disembodied head (and shoulders). He is not quite real, somehow, and seems almost a prop that talks, and talks, and talks.

Tamburlaine Also Tamburlane, Tamerlane. A Tartar conqueror of the 14th century.

Tara The O'Hara family's plantation in Margaret Mitchell's novel *Gone With the Wind* (1936) was named after the Hill of Tara, where the kings of ancient Ireland held sway.

Tea and Sympathy A play (1953) by Robert Anderson about a sensitive prep school student who is not accepted by the other students. It is the function of the headmaster's wife to offer

light refreshments and an understanding ear to all the boys who
are away from home, in her husband's charge, and she takes
particular interest in this one.

tell it (that) to the marines   Tell your story to someone
who is gullible enough to accept it ("—the sailors won't believe
it.")   —Sir Walter Scott,* *Redgauntlet.*

tempest in a teapot   Inside a teapot brought to the boil,
there is a violent, seething, turbulent storm of activity—but it
is, after all, only in a teapot, which is a trivial object.
—Proverb.

Ten Commandments   The rules of behavior set down by God
on two tablets of stone and given to Moses on Mt. Sinai. These
laws were the token of the covenant, or agreement, between God
and his people, the Israelites.   —Bible, Exod. 19–34.

"Ten Little Indians"   A rhyme about a group of little Indians
which is reduced in number, one by one, for various reasons (the
first simply "went home") until there was none left. Used as a
variant title of Agatha Christie's mystery novel *And Then There
Were None* (1957).

tender is the night   Transported by the intoxicating, enchanting power of his verse and the nightingale's haunting song, the
poet fancies that he is carried off with the bird into the lush, warm
darkness among the trees that it inhabits. As he muses on the
nightingale's immortality, remarking that the same song he hears

was heard "in ancient days," the poet is suddenly brought back to himself and forlornly listens as the song fades away in the distance. In 1934, F. Scott Fitzgerald* wrote a novel called *Tender is the Night*.   —John Keats,* "Ode to a Nightingale."

tender mercies   In the Old Testament's Book of Proverbs, this phrase is used ironically: "The tender mercies of the wicked are cruel" (12:10). It usually has this force when used today. On the other hand, when St. Luke refers to "the tender mercy of our God" (1:78), he is obviously quite sincere.

terrible swift sword   The weapon of justice and vengeance wielded by Jesus (actually, proceeding "out of his mouth") against the wicked of the earth in the last great battle at the end of the world. Title of the record volume (1963) of Bruce Catton's centennial history of the U.S. Civil War.   —Bible, Rev. 19:21.

"Thanatopsis"   A poem by William Cullen Bryant. In Greek, the title means "a view of death."

that it should come to this   No one could have foreseen that matters would work out in such a way—how shocking and terrible it is!   —William Shakespeare, *Hamlet,* act 1, sc. 2.

that last infirmity of noble mind   The desire for fame is characterized by the 17th century English poet as one illness which is fatal to an excellent and lofty mind.   —John Milton,* "Lycidas."

that way madness lies   Recalling his daughters' unkind treatment of him, King Lear attempts to thrust the thought away, for he fears it will make him insane with grief.   —William Shakespeare, *King Lear*, act 3, sc. 4.

their finest hour   Rallying the people of Great Britain to stand fast against the Nazi onslaught, the Prime Minister urges them to bear themselves so that ". . . if the British Empire . . . last for a thousand years, men will still say: 'This was their finest hour!'"   —Winston Churchill,* speech in the House of Commons on the day France surrendered to Germany.

theirs not to reason why   The British soldiers who are ordered to carry out a suicidal attack in the Battle of Balaclava (1854), are not entitled to question their orders; they must simply obey.   —Alfred, Lord Tennyson,* "The Charge of the Light Brigade."

there but for the grace of God go I   If you see someone doing wrong or suffering punishment for wrongdoing, you may feel smug and self-righteously superior; or you may humbly acknowledge that if God had not seen fit to help you, you would very likely be in that other person's place.   —attributed to the English Protestant martyr John Bradford (1510–1555).

there is a season   In the course of our existence, sooner or later there will be an occasion for "every purpose under the heaven"—a time to experience every emotion and perform every act of which humanity is capable, for better or worse.   —Bible, Eccles. 3:1.

They also serve The blind poet fears that because of his handicap, he will be unable to use the ability God gave him. Then he realizes that those "who only stand and wait" also serve God, if they bear their afflictions patiently.   —John Milton,* "On His Blindness."

they know not what they do In agony on the Cross, Jesus yet finds it in his heart to ask God to forgive those who are tormenting him, for they do not realize he is the son of God. —Bible, Luke 23:34.

they that go down to the sea in ships The psalmist says that sailors, who "do business in great waters," can testify to the wonders that God works. God raises the winds and waves, and the sailors are fearful; but when they appeal to God he saves them.   —Bible, Psa. 107:23.

they that take the sword shall perish with the sword Thus Jesus rebukes a disciple who strikes off the ear of one of the men who have arrested Jesus in the Garden of Gethsemane.   —Bible, Matt. 26:52.

they toil not, neither do they spin In his Sermon on the Mount, Jesus says one should not be preoccupied with getting food, clothing, and the like but rather with righteousness. God will provide the necessities of life for man, just as he provides glorious "clothing" for lilies, which do not toil or spin fiber into thread.   —Bible, Matt. 6:28.

thief in the night   St. Paul says that the day of the Lord —that is, the time of judgment, when wicked persons will have to pay for their sins—will come "like a thief in the night." It will be unexpected and sudden, and there will be no escape. —Bible, I Thess. 5:2.

thin red line, the   The rank of scarlet-clad British soldiers (the 93rd Highlanders) who, although badly outnumbered, held their ground against a Russian attack in the Battle of Balaclava, in the Crimean War of 1854. They were all that stood between the enemy and the British supply base at the port of Balaclava, and they fought in line because there was no time to form a square. Title of a novel (1962) by American author James Jones.

things fall apart   The poet feels that mankind is becoming fragmented, anarchic—that the fragile sense of a common destiny which has bound men together is giving way. Now, like a falcon which has flown too far from its trainer and "can no longer hear the falconer," men are spinning off in the chaotic maelstrom of war. The best men are disillusioned and impotent, "lack all conviction," and the worst, unfortunately, are filled with purpose and determination. It seems to the poet that "the Second Coming is at hand," and he has an ominous vision of the form it will take.   —William Butler Yeats.* "The Second Coming."   See also: the Second Coming.

things that go bump in the night   Frightening and unexplainable noises, apparently supernatural—in the same class as "ghoulies and ghosties and long-leggety beasties." —Scottish prayer.

think tank   A commercial institution, secure against distraction, in which persons of various intellectual disciplines immerse themselves in intensive thought, brainstorming and/or systematically pursuing specific lines of inquiry in an effort to solve problems, detect trends, and consider far-reaching possibilities.

Third Reich   The name given by Adolf Hitler to Germany under his dictatorship (1933–1945). According to Hitler, the Holy Roman Empire was the first Reich (Empire), the German Empire of Bismarck was the second, and his was the third.

third world   Those nations in Africa, Asia, and Latin America which emerged from colonial status after World War II and are not officially aligned with either the Western democracies or the Eastern communist bloc. (Of the other two "worlds," which one is considered first and which second, would depend on the point of view, but this is never at issue.)

thirty pieces of silver   Judas Iscariot, one of Jesus' apostles, betrayed his master to his enemies for a fee of thirty pieces of silver. Later, he regretted what he had done, and "he cast down the pieces of silver in the temple, and departed, and went and hanged himself."   —Bible, Matt. 26:15; 27:5.

this above all   Polonius, counselor to the king, tells his son Laertes how he should behave when he is abroad, concluding with the advice that above all he be true to himself. He means that Laertes must be honest with himself (which is not as easy as it sounds) and have the courage of his convictions. If he lives by this principle, Polonius says, he cannot "be false to any man." Title of a novel (1941) by Eric Knight. —William Shakespeare, *Hamlet,* act 1, sc. 3.

this happy breed John of Gaunt, Duke of Lancaster under King Richard II, intones his ringing, heartfelt praise of England and the "happy breed of men" which inhabits it—happy primarily in the sense that the English are blessed and fortunate to have the qualities that distinguish their racial stock. Title of a play later made into a film (1944) by Noel Coward. —William Shakespeare, *Richard II,* act 2, sc. 1.

this other Eden Thus old John of Gaunt, Duke of Lancaster, proudly describes the realm of England. It is, he says, a "demi-paradise, . . . little world, . . . blessed plot." Title of a novel (1977) by Marilyn Harris. —William Shakespeare, *Richard II,* act 2, sc. 1.

thorn in one's side An angel, speaking for God, tells the Israelites that because they have not thrown down the altars of the Canaanites—whose land they took with the help of God—the Canaanites and their gods shall remain "as thorns in [their] sides" —a constant, irritating source of discomfort and trouble. —Bible, Judg. 2:3.

thorns of life The tedious, toilsome, mundane aspects of day-to-day human existence. The poet, exhausted and discouraged, feels as though he is stumbling through a thicket of thorns; falling upon them, he is bled of his spiritual vitality. —Percy Bysshe Shelley,* "Ode to the West Wind."

thou hast said (it)   At the Last Supper, Jesus foretells his
betrayal by one of the Twelve Apostles who sit at the table with
him. When Judas asks, "Master, is it I?" Jesus replies, "Thou hast
said." Later, when the Roman governor Pilate asks him if he is
King of the Jews, Jesus says, "Thou sayest." Today, when one is
asked, "Do you mean to tell me. . .?", he may reply, *"You* said
it."—as if to say, "You have admitted the truth out of your own
mouth, and therefore I don't have to." If he adds, "—I didn't," he
may be hedging, evading a total commitment.   —Bible, Matt.
26:25; 27:11.

**thou shalt not muzzle the ox when he treadeth out
the corn**   One of various laws and ordinances laid down by
Moses when the Israelites were in the wilderness after their flight
from Egypt. It means that the animal that a farmer uses to thresh
wheat should be permitted to eat some of the kernels that its work
produces. The principle that one who labors for another should not
be denied some portions of the profits he produces may be applied
in various ways. St. Paul invokes it in his Epistle to the
Corinthians.   —Bible, Deut. 25:4; I Cor. 9:9.

Thousand and One Nights, The   Scheherazade, wife of
the sultan Schahriah, was able to induce him to postpone her
execution, night by night for 1,001 nights, by intriguing him daily
with one of these romantic Oriental stories. They are also known
as *The Arabian Nights Entertainments.*

Three Musketeers, The   A novel by Alexandre Dumas*
recounting the dashing exploits of Athos, Porthos and Aramis,
members of the company of mounted, musket-armed guardsmen
who served the kings of France in the 17th and 18th centuries.

Early in the novel, they are joined by young D'Artagnan. Their adventures are recounted in several other books by Dumas.

three score (years) and ten   Literally, seventy (three times a score, or twenty, equals sixty; then add ten). Roughly or on the average, the span of a human lifetime.   —Bible, Psalm 90:10.

through a glass darkly   St. Paul says that in this life, our knowledge is imperfect; if we perceive the truth, our vision is impaired, distorted, as if by an intervening pane of flawed or discolored glass.   —Bible, I Cor. 13:12.

throw down the gauntlet   According to the practice of medieval chivalry, if one knight stripped off his gauntlet, or glove, and threw it down at the feet of another, he was offering a challenge, inviting combat.

throw out the baby with the bath water   Keep the baby, by all means, when it has been bathed and the tub is emptied of the now useless, dirty water—that is, it would be absurd to destroy something good because it is flawed; rather, one should simply remove the flaws and retain what is good.

tiger by the tail   If one grasps a ferocious tiger by the tail, he *may* be able to avoid being mauled; but how long can he hold on?   See also: man on a tiger.

tiller of the ground/soil, a   A farmer. Cain, one of the sons of Adam, is so described. He was the first murderer.   —Bible, Gen. 4:2   See also: Cain.

tilting at windmills   The fictional character Don Quixote is a senile old man who imagines himself to be a brave young knight in shining armor. Believing it to be a giant, he attacks a windmill with his "lance" and is almost killed as a result. Therefore, any one-sided, hopeless or idealistic battle would be an example of tilting at windmills.   —Miguel de Cervantes,* *Don Quixote,* See also: Quixotic.

time and the hour runs through the roughest day   No matter how difficult it may be to endure a period of hopeful waiting, time *will* pass.   —William Shakespeare, *Macbeth,* act 1, sc. 3.

time and the river   According to the Roman emperor and Stoic philosopher Marcus Aurelius (A.D. 121–180), the river of time sweeps one thing along and replaces it with another which also shall be carried away. *Of Time and the River* is a novel (1935) by Thomas Wolfe.*   —*Meditations.*

time is a river   That is, a stream "of passing events" which, having brought one event to occur, immediately sweeps it away and replaces it with another.   —Marcus Aurelius, *Meditations.*

time out of mind   Dating from so long ago that no one can remember—it has slipped out of the mind. Title of a novel (1935) by Rachael Field.   —William Shakespeare, *Romeo and Juliet,* act 1, sc. 4.

time's winged chariot The poet pictures time as the driver of an all too speedy chariot—perhaps the Greek sun-god Apollo, who drove such a vehicle across the sky each day. He hears it relentlessly "hurrying near" and sees before him "deserts of vast eternity."   —Andrew Marvell,* *To His Coy Mistress.*

Tin-Pan Alley Not literally an alley or even a specific street, but the district in New York City where most popular music publishers are found. It used to be in the vicinity of 14th Street.

Titans Offspring of Earth (Gaea) by Sky (Uranus). The Titan Cronus deposed his father Uranus and was in turn deposed by one of his own sons, Zeus, who became chief of the Olympian gods and cast the Titans into Tartarus, under the earth.

to bury Caesar Mark Antony's stated purpose in appearing before the Roman people after Caesar's assassination. He adds that he is not there to praise Caesar, but in fact he is. —William Shakespeare, *Julius Caesar,* act 3, sc. 2.

to buy the Brooklyn Bridge To be played for a sucker. It used to be said that a big city slicker could pick up a nice piece of change by convincing credulous country boys that they could buy that famous structure from him for a song.

to catch a thief The best way to do this is to "set a thief"—i.e., employ someone who, being a thief, is familiar with a thief's methods, and set him, like a trap, to capture the one you are after. Title of an Alfred Hitchcock film (1955).

to have and have not   According to the writer, "There are only two families [i.e., classes] in the world," those who have property and power, and those who don't. Title of a novel (1937) by Ernest Hemingway.*   —Miquel de Cervantes,* *Don Quixote.*

to the manner born   Qualified to recognize customary ways of behavior in a certain region because one was born and raised there.   —William Shakespeare, *Hamlet,* act 1, sc. 4.

to reap what you sow   What crop a farmer reaps depends, of course, on the kind of seeds he plants. Similarly, if a man devotes himself to things of this world he will be corrupted, as all things of this world must decay; if he devotes himself to the spirit, he will live forever.   —Bible, Gal. 6:7.

to see ourselves as others see us   Every man has an image of himself, but other people's impressions of him may be quite different. Here the poet says that if we could see ourselves as others do, we would be less likely to blunder and entertain foolish notions. The case in point is a lady who thinks everyone is staring at her because she is so attractive; in fact, they are fascinated by the sight of a louse crawling over her bonnet.   —Robert Burns,* "To a Louse."

To strive, to seek, to find, and not to yield   —See: I am a part of all that I have met.

Toby Belch   An old, fat, jolly, reckless, fun-loving knight. His favorite companion is an excessively thin old gentleman named Sir Andrew Aguecheek.   —William Shakespeare, *Twelfth Night*.

tongues of fire   On the day of Pentecost, all eleven of Jesus' Apostles had gathered together, when "there appeared unto them cloven tongues like as of fire" which "sat upon each of them. And they were all filled with the Holy Ghost, and began to speak with other tongues." Thus they were enabled to preach to all nations.   —Bible, Acts 2:3.

torch singer   A vocalist who specializes in songs about disappointed love. She musically "carries the torch" of steadfast love for one who does not love her.

Torquemada   Grand Inquisitor General of Spain in the late 15th century. His pious devotion to the Catholic faith and powers of organization eminently qualified him to carry out the cruel practices of the Spanish Inquisition, in the course of which tens of thousands were tried and many tortured and/or executed.

tower of Babel   Generations after Noah, all people still spoke one language. Out of pride they began to build a lofty tower, and God confused their language and scattered them so they would not be able to unite and pose a threat to him. Thus *Babel* suggests a confused noise of voices.   —Bible, Gen. 11:1–9.

tragic flaw   Some fatal flaw in the character of a person who, if he is not exceptionally good, is no villain either; in classic and Elizabethan tragedy this person has eminent status. The flaw leads relentlessly to the destruction of everything that makes this person's life meaningful, and often to his death.   —Aristotle,* *Poetics.*

tree of knowledge   The tree "in the midst of the garden" of Eden, actually the tree of knowledge of good and evil. God told Adam not to eat the fruit of this tree. When he and Eve did so, they lost their innocence, and God drove them out of the garden. —Bible, Gen. 2–3   See also: Adam; Eden; Eve; tree of life.

tree of life   A tree in the garden of Eden. If Adam and Eve had eaten its fruit they would have become immortal.   —Bible, Gen. 3:22.   See also: Adam; Eden; Eve; tree of knowledge.

Trilby   Heroine of the novel (1894) by the same name, a girl with a magnificent singing voice who, unfortunately, is tone-deaf—i.e., her ear is insensitive to the differences in pitch of the notes she sings. Under the sinister influence of the hypnotist Svengali, she is capable of singing beautifully; when he dies, the spell is broken, and she is released.   —George du Maurier.   See also: Svengali.

trimmed lamp, a   —See: wise and foolish virgins, the.

troglodyte   From the Greek for "cave dweller." Figuratively, anyone who is out of touch with contemporary developments.

Troilus and Cressida   Troilus and Cressida were figures in the Trojan War, but the story of their love is of medieval origin, Chaucer's* and Shakespeare's versions being the best known.

Troilus was a Trojan prince, and Cressida the daughter of the Greek soothsayer Calchas. When she was repatriated, she swore to be true to Troilus but betrayed him.   See also: Pandarus.

Trojan horse   In the epic siege of the city of Troy, the Greeks fashioned a huge wooden horse which was, they said, an offering to Athene so that they would have a good journey back to Greece; the Trojans, convinced the Greeks were leaving, dragged it inside their walls. In fact, the whole thing was a ruse. The horse contained a detachment of Greek soldiers who emerged after dark and opened the city gates to let the rest of their army in. Thus Troy was defeated and put to the torch after withstanding the assaults of their enemies for so many years.   —Homer,* *The Odyssey.*

Trojan War   The ten-year conflict between the Greeks and the city of Troy in Asia Minor. It was touched off when Paris, Prince of Troy, carried off the legendary beauty Helen, wife of King Menelaus of Sparta. Homer* and Virgil* tell of this siege in their epic poems the *Iliad* and the *Aeneid,* respectively; the tale may be based on actual occurrences some 1100 to 1200 years before Christ.

trout in the milk   Circumstantial evidence can be very strong. In the old days, milk was peddled from door to door in large tin cans. Finding a fish in one's milk would certainly make one suspicious that the milk had been watered down.   —Henry David Thoreau,* *Journal.*

turn the other cheek   In the Sermon on the Mount, Jesus refers to the Old Testament principle of "an eye for an eye," which means that if one is injured he should get even, and says that we should not resist evil; rather, if one is struck on one cheek, he should meekly present the other cheek to the offender. —Bible, Matt. 5:39.

Tweedledum and Tweedledee   A very unusual set of fat and clumsy twin boys who are mirror images of one another, and agree to fight over a broken rattle. The fight, however, never takes place.   —Lewis Carroll,* Through the Looking-Glass.

twelve good men   A jury.   —Lord Brougham.

Twelve Tribes, the   —See: Joseph.

twig in the river   Time has been compared to a river, which implies that one can go back in time just as it is possible to go upstream. If one does go upstream in time and figuratively drops a twig into that river—i.e., does some trivial thing which was not done originally at that point in time—then theoretically that twig may be enough to start a logjam, thus altering the flow of the stream from that point on, which would have an incalculable effect on the circumstances which exist in the present. This theory is discussed at length in Jack Finney's novel Time and Again (1970).

Twilight of the Gods   The Ragnarok or Gotterdammerung. The gods of Norse mythology, it was believed, were doomed to meet their enemies, the forces of evil, in a last, cataclysmic battle—and lose. Norse heroes who died bravely in mortal combat were entitled to sit in Valhalla, one of the halls of the gods, until the day of Ragnarok, when they would have the privilege of fighting alongside their gods and dying with them in that hopeless struggle.

two by two   —See: Noah's Ark.

Tyger! Tyger!   —See: burning bright.

U

ugly duckling   Someone who is at first scorned or unappreciated, but whose true worth is eventually discovered. In the children's tale, a small "duckling" is mocked and derided by his peers until he matures into a beautiful swan.   —Hans Christian Andersen.*

ultima Thule   The northernmost land mass known in ancient times, supposedly six days by ship north of Britain—for all practical purposes, the very edge of the world.

Ulysses   The Latin modification of the Greek *Odysseus*. Title of a novel by James Joyce in which the one day's movements of Leopold Bloom, an ordinary Dubliner, parallel the ten years' wandering of Odysseus recounted in Homer's* *Odyssey*. Joyce uses the stream of consciousness technique in depicting Bloom's moment-by-moment experiences.   See also: Odysseus.

Uncle Tom's Cabin   Harriet Beecher Stowe's* inflammatory novel (Lincoln said it touched off the Civil War) dramatizing the evils of slavery. The fact that Mr. St. Clare, who owns the title character, is kindly does little to excuse the injustice of that institution. The term "Uncle Tom" has come to mean a black who cooperates with whites in an attempt to win their approval.   See also: Simon Legree.

under a cloud   The cloud represents uncertainty, perhaps even suspicion, about the one who lives under it: he is not clearly above reproach.

undiscover'd country, the   The realm on the other side of death, undiscovered in that no one who goes there ever returns to tell what it is like. It is the uncertainty about this, Prince Hamlet muses—the dread that it may be worse there than here—that deters us from suicide.   —William Shakespeare, *Hamlet*, act 3, sc. 1.

Uneasy lies the head that wears a crown.   King Henry IV, busy with worrisome affairs of state in the middle of the night—he is in his nightgown—envies common people who can sleep soundly at such an hour. Kings and Queens do not have that privilege because of the responsibilities that weigh upon them and because of the ruthless and ambitious persons who are always looking for an opportunity to seize the throne.   —William Shakespeare, *Henry IV*, Part II, act 3, sc. 1.

unicorn   A fabulous animal, basically equine in form, whose most distinguishing characteristic is a long, straight, often spiral horn in the middle of its forehead.

untouchables   A hereditary caste in India, once segregated, who the Hindus believed would defile those of a higher caste who came into contact with them.

up the river   Where many notorious felons convicted in New York were sent when Sing Sing was in its prime as a maximum security prison. It is located at Ossining, up the Hudson River from New York City.

Uriah Heep   A clerk who makes a great show of humility—he is continually protesting that he is "'umble"—but is in fact a malicious and conniving sneak who resorts to blackmail. —Charles Dickens,* *David Copperfield*.

Utopia   Title of a 16th century book describing a place where society and life are perfect. It is a Greek word which means "no place."   —Sir Thomas More.   See also: Cloud-Cuckoo Land; Eden; Paradise; Shangri-La.

V

valley of death   The valley through which the British Light Cavalry Brigade charged to its destruction in the Battle of Balaclava in 1854. The phrase was probably adapted from the twenty-third Psalm, which refers to "the valley of the shadow of death."
—Alfred, Lord Tennyson,* "The Charge of the Light Brigade."

valley of decision   The valley of Jehoshaphat, where God will meet the heathen enemies of Israel on the day of final judgment and visit his wrath upon those who have pillaged Judah.   —Bible, Joel 3:14.

Vanity Fair   A sort of bazaar sponsored by several prominent devils in the town of Vanity in John Bunyan's allegorical *The Pilgrim's Progress* (1678–1684). On exhibit and available for a price (ultimately, they cost one his soul) are sundry vanities—i.e., influences, properties and worldly pleasures. Title of a novel (1848) by William Makepeace Thackeray.*

veil of the Temple   —See: holy of holies.

veni, vidi, vici   —See: I came, I saw, I conquered.

viewless wings of poesy, the An image suggesting the enchanting power of poetry: reading, hearing or composing it, one soars, as on invisible wings, above the "leaden-eyed despairs" of human experience. Verse, says the poet, is more intoxicating than wine.   —John Keats,* "Ode to a Nightingale."

virgin shall conceive, a —and bear a son, and shall call his name Immanuel. The famous prophecy which was later interpreted as a reference to the Messiah, specifically Jesus. Actually, the birth referred to was intended as a sign to the king (Ahaz) who reigned at the time the prophecy was made, and it occurred in his lifetime.   —Bible, Isa. 7:14.

Virtue is its own reward. According to Silius Italicus (c. 25–A.D. 99), "Virtue herself is her own fairest reward"—i.e., one should not expect to profit from doing what is right; he should be satisfied simply with the knowledge that he has acted virtuously.

voice crying in the wilderness, a A warning or important announcement proclaimed to those who will not listen. John the Baptist preached in the wilderness of Judah, urging repentance: "for the kingdom of heaven is at hand." This had been prophesied by Isaiah.   —Bible, Isaiah 40:3; Matt. 3:3.

voice of the people, the —is the voice of God (Latin: *vox populi, vox Dei*); therefore, a ruler should heed it. —Alcuin, letter to Charlemagne.

voice of the turtle The turtledove, that is. When it is heard, one can be sure that spring has come. Title of a play (1944) by the English-born American dramatist John Van Druten.   —Bible, Song of Solomon 2:12.

Volpone Title character in Ben Jonson's comic play (1606). His name means "fox," and he is as wily as he is avaricious, perpetrating an elaborate hoax to separate several vulturous acquaintances from their riches.

von Clausewitz Prussian general (1780–1831), author of *On War*, a book in which he sets forth his philosophy on military conflict and outlines principles of warfare which are still applicable—e.g., the definition of war as "a continuation of policy by other means."

W

wages of sin Death is the "pay-off" for those who commit sins.   —Bible, Romans 6:23.

wailing wall All that remains of the reconstructed second Temple in Jerusalem, a section of the outer western wall which may contain stones of Solomon's original Temple. Here Jews gather to lament the destruction of those Temples and the scattering of the people of Israel. More broadly, anyone to whom one tells his troubles is a wailing wall.

Waiting for Godot In the play of this title (1952), the two major characters keep showing up for a promised meeting with the mysterious Godot (perhaps representing God), who never does make an appearance. —Samuel Beckett.

waiting for the other shoe to fall Waiting for the other person (who has just said or done something) to finish what he has started. The saying signifies that one is being kept in suspense until he hears or sees what is to follow.

Walden Pond A small body of water in Massachusetts on the shores of which author Henry David Thoreau* lived a simple life for several years. He wrote a book about his experiences and his reflections on nature called *Walden* (1854).

walking on water A miraculous feat accomplished by Jesus. Peter attempted to follow his Master but began to sink; Jesus attributed this to his lack of faith. Anyone described as walking on water is being compared to Jesus. —Bible, Matt. 14:25.

walls of Jericho God told Joshua, successor of Moses, to lead the Israelites into Canaan and march about the city of Jericho. When they had done this, the priests blew their trumpets, and all the people shouted. The walls of Jericho fell flat, and the Israelites took the city. —Bible, Josh. 6. See also: land flowing with milk and honey; Moses.

Walter Mitty   Central figure in the story "The Secret Life of Walter Mitty" by James Thurber (1894–1961); he is a timid, middle-aged man who enriches his humdrum existence by daydreaming. He imagines himself as a daring flyer, a surgeon, a naval hero, a spy, etc., while on a shopping trip with his henpecking wife.

wandering Jew   In medieval legend, a Jew who refused to allow Jesus to rest at his door while he was carrying his cross to Calvary. He was a shoemaker named Ahasuerus, and for this treatment of the Son of God he was condemned to wander over the face of the earth until Judgment Day.

War Between Men and Women, The   A series of cartoons by James Thurber depicting an imaginary war taking place between the two sexes. Although the series is essentially humorous, this same concept runs through so much of the literary and artistic output of its creator that it might well represent one of his major themes.

war to end all wars   A reference to World War I (1914–1918). It was optimistically hoped that this would indeed be the final bloody struggle, after which the world would be united in peace. It is difficult to discover who first used the expression, although it is often associated with President Woodrow Wilson.

Wars of the Roses   A series of 15th century civil wars, lasting for thirty years, in which the house of York (represented by a white rose) and the house of Lancaster (red rose) contended for the throne of England. The outcome was the crowning of Henry VII.

warts and all Including in one's depiction of another person, even that person's imperfections—showing him exactly as he really is. The English Lord Protector Oliver Cromwell (1595–1658) said to a painter who was beginning work on Cromwell's portrait, "I desire you would . . . paint my picture truly like me; . . . remark all these roughnesses, pimples, warts, and everything as you see me . . ." —Horace Walpole (1717–1797), *Anecdotes of Painting.*

washed in the blood of the lamb In the dream-vision of St. John the Divine, those who have suffered for Christ (and been redeemed by his sacrificial death) appear in white robes which have been washed in Christ's blood, and God will live in their midst. —Bible, Rev. 7:14–17.

"Waste Land, The" Title of a long poem written in 1922; the waste land is a sterile area, blighted by a curse, where no crops will grow. The author was symbolizing his concept of the spiritual sterility of the 20th century. The work is filled with quotations and allusions from a variety of religious and literary works of the past, and contains copious explanatory notes appended to the poem by the author. —T. S. Eliot.

watchful waiting President Woodrow Wilson coined this phrase in stating our policy toward Mexico in 1915 when our relations with that country were in a doubtful condition.

water from a rock When the Israelites were suffering from thirst in the wilderness after their departure from Egypt, God told Moses to strike a rock with his rod. Moses struck the rock twice,

and an abundance of water came out.   —Bible, Num.
20:1–11.

water, water everywhere   In a mystical romantic ballad,
an old sailor tells how his ship was becalmed in the middle of the
ocean, and the men, extremely thirsty, were surrounded by water,
none of it drinkable. The actual quotation is "Water, water, every
where,/Nor any drop to drink."   —Samuel Taylor Coleridge,* "The Rime of the Ancient Mariner."

way of all flesh, the   An expression from a 17th century
play denoting that, when all is said and done, the human fleshly
passions and appetites will be followed. The phrase was used as
the title of a novel (1903) by Samuel Butler, a realistic, bitter
study of narrow-mindedness and hypocrisy.   —Thomas
Dekker and John Webster, *Westward Ho!* (1607).

We are not amused.   Queen Victoria's regally dignified
expression of disapproval when she witnessed an imitation of her
by her groom-in-waiting. Traditionally a monarch refers to
himself/herself with the plural pronouns as a mark of distinction.   See also: royal we.

We have nothing to fear but fear itself.   —See: only
thing we have to fear is fear itself.

We who are about to die salute you.   Traditional
salutation of gladiators to their emperor before going to do battle
(to the death) in the arena.

wedding guest An unnamed person who is stopped, as he is entering a church to attend a wedding, by an old seafarer who tells him a long story, in verse form, about a sailor who shot an albatross, bringing bad luck to his shipmates.   —Samuel Taylor Coleridge,* "The Rime of the Ancient Mariner." See also: albatross; ancient mariner.

weeping and gnashing of teeth Signs of remorse, regret, anguish, etc., evidenced by lost sinners in hell.   —Bible, Matt. 25:30.

weird sisters In William Shakespeare's *Macbeth*, three strange women who dress and behave like witches, and who make prophecies to Macbeth about his future. All of these prophecies come true, but not in the ways Macbeth has assumed. Some scholars feel that they are actual witches, gifted with supernatural powers; others are of the opinion that they are crazed women who only imagine themselves to be witches.

What the dickens "Dickens," a corruption of "devilkins" (little devils), was in common usage as a mild swear word hundreds of years before the birth of England's great novelist, Charles Dickens.*   —William Shakespeare, *The Merry Wives of Windsor*.

What is truth? Pontius Pilate's question, put to Jesus when Jesus had been brought before him for questioning. It suggests the impossibility of determining the nature of anything so abstract as the "truth," as Jesus uses the term.   —Bible, John 18:38.

What manner of man is this? The question asked by Jesus' awed disciples after he had calmed the wind and sea during a fearful storm. —Bible, Mark 4:41.

What Price Glory? A play (1924) by Maxwell Anderson set in France during World War I. The title asks how much the glory in battle that some men strive for will cost in terms of suffering and death.

What's Hecuba to him . . . Hamlet is struck with awe and admiration for an actor who has wept real tears while describing the tragedy of Hecuba, a character appearing in tales of the Trojan War. Hamlet finds it amazing that this actor can show such emotion over the fate of this fictional character. "What's Hecuba to him or he to Hecuba/That he should weep for her?" —William Shakespeare, *Hamlet,* act 2, sc. 2.

what's past is prologue Sebastian, brother of the King of Naples, is urged to kill his brother and take his place. The instigator says that if Sebastian seizes this opportunity, the order of the past and Sebastian's place in that order—i.e., in the shadow of his brother—will be merely an introduction to the future, which it will be in Sebastian's power to control. —William Shakespeare, *The Tempest,* act 2, sc. 1.

Whatsoever thy hand findeth to do, do it with thy might . . . Anything worth doing is worth doing well; put your heart into your work. —Bible, Eccles, 9:10.

Wheel of Fortune Fortuna, the classic goddess of chance, was usually depicted as blind and with a wheel, symbolizing her ever-changing nature. This wheel of fortune was, in medieval times, a much-used symbol in art and literature.

wheels within wheels The complexity of life. In the original, Ezekiel saw a vision of heavenly visitors propelled by some mode of transportation involving "a wheel in the middle of a wheel." In modern times, however, the expression has come to refer to a system, organization, device, etc., in which various factors, interlocking and interdependent, combine to make a complicated structure.

when in Rome One should adopt the customs or habits of one's surroundings; popularly worded as: "When in Rome, do as the Romans do." Attributed to English churchman and scholar Robert Burton (1577–1640). —*The Anatomy of Melancholy.*

when it rains, it pours Troubles don't seem to come one at a time; to many it appears that "bad luck comes in bunches." Sometimes stated: "It never rains but it pours."

when the saints go marching in In his dream-vision, St. John the Divine is told that after the second coming of Christ, the saints—those who suffered for their faith—would go into "the beloved city" of Jerusalem and reign with Christ for a thousand years. At the end of that millennium, following the Last Judgment, *all* of those who followed God's Commandments would enter the heavenly Jerusalem. —Bible, Rev. 20:4–9; 22:14.

When she was good   —that is, the little girl "Who had a little curl/Right in the middle of her forehead"—"She was very, very good,/But when she was bad she was horrid."   —Henry Wadsworth Longfellow,* "There Was a Little Girl."

where there's smoke . . .   . . . there's fire. Certain forms of evidence seem to be overwhelming proof. Signs of smoke usually indicate the presence of a fire.   See also: trout in the milk.

which side his bread is buttered on   A person who knows which side of his bread is buttered will not make the mistake of putting that side down. In fact he will not make the mistake of doing anything which is not in his own interest.   —John Heywood, *Proverbs.*

whipping boy   It used to be the custom in certain countries for the heir to the throne, while a young lad, to have a boy of his age employed to be whipped when the prince committed some naughty deed. This "whipping boy" thus bore the burden of the punishment in the place of his young master, who, being of royal blood, was immune from physical punishment. Thus, someone suffering the consequences of another's misdeeds may be termed a whipping boy.

whistling in the dark   Attempting to keep up a show of bravery or indifference in a frightening or dangerous situation. From the play *Amphitryon,* by John Dryden (1631–1700).

White Knight   A gentle, chivalrous but clumsy and confused old fellow whom Alice encounters in her progress across the chessboard world on the other side of her looking glass. He repeatedly falls off his horse; when he is not flat on his back or head over heels, he tells her of the many nonsensical things he has invented, like pudding made from blotting paper.   —Lewis Carroll,* *Through the Looking-Glass.*

white man's burden   The heavy and difficult duty, which the white race was supposedly obligated to bear, of bringing civilization to backward colored peoples. This pious but presumptuous phrase was often used to justify the exploitation of those peoples.   —Rudyard Kipling,* "The White Man's Burden."

whited sepulchres   One of the scathing epithets with which Christ addresses the scribes and Pharisees. (He also calls them hypocrites and a "generation of vipers.") He means that they are like beautifully decorated tombs which contain "dead men's bones, and . . . uncleanness."   —Bible, Matt. 23:27.

"Whither thou goest . . .   . . . I will go"—so said Ruth to her mother-in-law Naomi when Naomi decided to return to Judah after the death of Ruth's husband and brother-in-law. Despite Naomi's protests that she would be better off staying in her native country, Ruth steadfastly insisted on going with her.   —Bible, Ruth 1:16.   See also: alien corn.

Who will free me from this turbulent priest?   England's King Henry II appointed his friend Thomas Becket (often referred to as Thomas à Becket) Archbishop of Canterbury in 1162, believing that he could depend on Becket to endorse whatever he did. To his surprise and anger, Becket took his responsibility very seriously and refused to permit Henry to infringe upon the prerogatives of the Church. It is said that, out of patience, Henry made this remark to several of his barons. They took him at his word and murdered Becket before the altar of Canterbury Cathedral. Becket later was canonized.

—whose ox is gored   It all depends on your viewpoint. If your ox is injured, you will be more upset than you would be if it were someone else's animal.   —Martin Luther, *Works.*

wicked flee when no man pursueth   A guilty person may be afraid of being found out, and thus run away to escape detection even if no one is actually after him.   —Bible, Prov. 28:1.

widow's mite   A small contribution or offering from someone who is unable to give much.   —Bible, Mark 12:42.

Wife of Bath   A jovial, bold, somewhat deaf woman who has been married five times; she is one of the tale-telling travelers in Chaucer's *Canterbury Tales.* The wife of Bath's tale focuses on the question, "What does a woman like best?" and deals with a knight of King Arthur's court who goes in search of the answer to this query. At last, he learns the answer: "To have her own sweet way."   —Geoffrey Chaucer,* *The Canterbury Tales.*

wild surmise   —See: silent, upon a peak in Darien.

willing suspension of disbelief   That "which constitutes poetic faith." It is the acknowledgment by the reader that, although

Willy Loman

what he is reading is not true, he will go along with whatever the author has to tell him as if he in fact *did* believe it to be true.   —Samuel Taylor Coleridge,* *Biographia Literaria.*

Willy Loman   Central character in a great 20th century tragic drama. He is a middle-aged traveling salesman who has managed to get along by being amiable and outgoing with his customers, but now finds that everything in his life—his job, family relationships, faith in himself—is coming undone.   —Arthur Miller,* *Death of a Salesman.*

Win this one for the Gipper.   A line from the 1940 movie *Knute Rockne—All American* about the famous Notre Dame football coach. George Gipp (played by Ronald Reagan), Rockne's star player, dies, and just before the big game, Rockne addresses the team in the locker room. He concludes his talk with this remark, and the team, inspired, wins against the odds.

The wine-dark sea   Homer's* often repeated description of the ocean, used in his epic poems the *Iliad* and the *Odyssey.*

wink at it   To condone wrongdoing, to be figuratively blind to a wrongful act.

winter of our discontent, the   Richard, Duke of York, exults that the long, bleak period during which his family has been out of power has been replaced by the "glorious summer" of his brother's accession to the throne of England. This follows the Yorkists' defeat of the Lancastrians in the War of the Roses (1471).

Title of a novel (1961) by John Steinbeck.*   —William
Shakespeare, *Richard III*, act 1, sc. 1.

wisdom of Solomon   King Solomon asked God for an
understanding heart, and his wisdom is exemplified in the case of
two women who claimed the same child. Solomon ordered that the
child be cut in half. When one of the women pleaded with him to
give it to the other rather than kill it, Solomon knew who was
telling the truth. He reputedly wrote the Book of Proverbs and the
Song of Solomon.   —Bible, I Kings 3:16—28; 4:29—34;
Proverbs.   See also: Queen of Sheba; Solomon.

wise and foolish virgins, the   In a parable, Jesus tells of
five wise virgins and five foolish ones. The foolish ones find it
necessary to trim (add fuel to) the lamps with which they will greet
the bridegroom, but they have not had the foresight to bring any
oil. While they are buying it, the other five go in to the marriage,
and the door is closed. The lesson of the parable is that one should
always watch and be prepared for the Second Coming.
—Bible, Matt. 25:1—13.

witch of Endor   King Saul, preparatory to going into a fateful
battle, consulted the sorceress known as the witch of Endor. She
conjured up the spirit of the prophet Samuel, who predicted the
coming defeat and death of Saul.   —Bible, I Sam. 28:7—14.

wolf in sheep's clothing   Jesus warns his followers to
"beware of false prophets, which come to you in sheep's clothing,
but inwardly they are ravening [starving] wolves." That is,
someone dangerous might seem to be harmless. "The Wolf in

Sheep's Clothing" is one of Aesop's* fables.   —Bible, Matt.
7:15.

(The) woman I love   British King Edward VIII gave up his
throne in 1936, in order to marry a twice-divorced American,
Walli. Warfield Simpson. His abdication speech included the
words: ". . . I have found it impossible . . . to discharge my duties
as King . . . without the help and support of the woman I love."

Wonderland   A dream world underground where all kinds of
absurd, fantastic things occur.   —Lewis Carroll,* *Alice in
Wonderland.*   See also: looking-glass world; Never-Never Land.

Woolf, Virginia   English novelist (1882—1941). Many of her
novels and stories exemplify the stream-of-consciousness technique
and, as a natural consequence, show how formidable is one's
inward sense of reality as opposed to external reality. The play
Who's Afraid of Virginia Woolf? (1962) was written by Edward
Albee.

word to the wise is sufficient, a   One who is wise need not
be told often or at length before he gets the message. "Good wits
jump" with a minimum of prompting.   —Miguel de Cervantes,* *Don Quixote.*

world enough and time   The poet tells his hesitant lover
that if they had "world enough, and time," her shyness would not
make any difference; as it is, though, he hears "time's winged
chariot hurrying near." They are mortal and must seize their

pleasure while they can. Title of a novel (1950) by Robert Penn Warren.   —Andrew Marvell,* "To his Coy Mistress."   See also: gather ye rosebuds while ye may.

world, the flesh and the devil, the   Material things of this world (as contrasted with the spiritual), pleasures of the flesh or senses, and utter evil.   —*The Book of Common Prayer.*

world's my oyster, the   Statement signifying that the speaker expects to extract profit from the world, just as one would obtain a valuable pearl from an oyster.   —William Shakespeare, *The Merry Wives of Windsor,* act 2, sc. 2.

wormwood   Common name for the aromatic herbs of the genus *Artemisia.* According to legend, the plant sprang up in the track of the serpent as it dragged itself along the ground after being forced out of Eden. Figuratively the word denotes bitterness.

worth one's salt   In ancient times, salt was widely used not only as a seasoning but as a preservative and an antiseptic. It was not easy to obtain, however, so it had considerable value and was used like money. Some people—Roman legionnaires, for example—were paid in salt (thus the word salary); in some places it was minted into coins. To be worth one's salt, therefore, was to earn the money one was paid.

wrong side of the blanket   This old expression refers to an illegitimate child, "born on the wrong side of the blanket."

wrong side of the tracks   —See: other side of the tracks.

X–Y–Z

Xanadu   A region straddling Europe and Asia, envisioned by the poet as the site of Kubla Khan's magnificent palace, "a stately pleasure dome." The name has connotations of mystery and romance.   —Samuel Taylor Coleridge,* "Kubla Khan."

Yahoo   On his fourth voyage, Lemuel Gulliver comes to the land of the Houyhnhnms, who, although they have the appearance of horses, are eminently reasonable. They are served by a race of detestable creatures called Yahoos, who have a disturbing resemblance to human beings. Thus a Yahoo is a base, ignorant person, devoid of decency and culture.   —Jonathan Swift,* *Gulliver's Travels.*

ye that pipe and ye that play   The poet is unable to "give [himself] up to jollity" like the "happy Shepherd-boy," who is closer in time to his glorious origin—God. Nevertheless, he can remember how he felt as a boy, when it was May, and joins, in thought, the birds that "pipe" and the lambs that play.   —William Wordsworth,* "Ode: Intimations of Immortality."

yellow brick road   The path that will lead one to the realization of his dreams. In L. Frank Baum's novel *Wonderful Wizard of Oz*

(1900), Dorothy, the Tin Woodman, the Scarecrow, and the Cowardly Lion follow this road to reach the Wizard in the hope that he will grant them their several desires.

yellow journalism Around the turn of the century, William Randolph Hearst's *New York Journal*, engaged in a circulation battle with other dailies, wooed readers with a lurid and sensational style and various kinds of features, including comics. This style became associated with one of the comic strips run in that newspaper, *The Yellow Kid.*

yellow peril The supposed danger that the Chinese and Japanese populations might eventually increase to the extent that these peoples, who were considered savagely inimical to the white races, would overrun the world.

Yes, Virginia, there *is* a Santa Claus. When a little girl named Virginia O'Hanlon wrote to the *New York Sun* that some of her friends did not believe in Santa Claus, the editor published his reply assuring her that they were wrong, that they had been "affected by the skepticism of a skeptical age." His reply epitomizes the idea that it is not necessary to see something in order to believe it.   —Francis P. Church (1839–1906), editorial.

yet a little while Jesus tells the people that he, the light, will be with them for a short time before he is ". . . lifted up from the earth," and that they should profit while they can from the light of understanding which he provides. The psalmist also uses this phrase: soon, he says, "the wicked shall not be."   —Bible, John 12:35; Psa. 37:10.

you can't get blood from a turnip   Some things just cannot be done, regardless of persistence, strength, virtue, etc. In the words of the 19th century English novelist: "There's no getting blood out of a turnip."   —Frederick Marryat, *Japhet in Search of a Father.*

you must pay the piper   Or else. The Pied Piper agreed to rid Hamelin of its rats for a fee. When the people balked at paying after the job was done, the Piper led all the town's children away. The same principle applies if the piper has been hired to play music for dancing. So says one of the characters in William Congreve's* play *Love for Love* (1695).   —German folktale.

young lions, the   The young warriors of other nations whom God has permitted to conquer and sack Jerusalem because the Jews have forsaken him. Title of a novel (1948) by Irwin Shaw.   —Bible, Jer. 2:15.

You're a better man than I am   An Englishman's poetic tribute to an Indian (i.e., from India) whose duty was to fetch water for the British soldiers. When the lowly Gunga Din performed an act of heroism, he won the man-to-man respect of the troops who usually despised the water bearers as mere servants.   —Rudyard Kipling* "Gunga Din."

Zion   Originally, a Jebusite fortress besieged and taken by David. Around this, "the city of David," grew the city of Jerusalem, with the whole of which Zion is often identified.

Appendix

Aesop (7th–6th centuries B.C.). Greek fabulist.

Andersen, Hans Christian (1805–1875). Danish poet, novelist, dramatist; best known as writer of fairy tales.

Aristotle (384–322 B.C.). Greek philosopher; pupil of Plato; tutor of Alexander the Great.

Bacon, Francis (1561–1626). English philosopher, statesman, essayist.

Balzac, Honoré de (1799–1850). French novelist; author of *La Comédie Humaine (The Human Comedy).*

Barrie, Sir J[ames] M[atthew] (1860–1937). Scottish novelist and dramatist; author of the play *Peter Pan.*

Blake, William (1757–1827). English poet and artist.

Boswell, James (1740–1795). Scottish lawyer and biographer; author of *The Life of Samuel Johnson, LL.D.*

Browning, Elizabeth Barrett (1806–1861). English poet; wife of Robert Browning.

Browning, Robert (1812–1889). English poet.

Burns, Robert (1759–1796). Scottish poet.

Byron, George Gordon (1788–1824). Called Lord Byron. English romantic poet.

Carroll, Lewis (pen name of Charles Lutwidge Dodgson) (1832–1898). English author, mathematician and photographer; author of *Alice's Adventures in Wonderland* and *Through the Looking-Glass*.

Cervantes [Saavedra], Miguel de (1547–1616). Spanish novelist, dramatist, and poet; author of the novel *Don Quixote*.

Chaucer, Geoffrey (c. 1343–1400). English poet; considered one of the most important writers of Middle English. Author of *The Canterbury Tales*.

Churchill, Sir Winston (1874–1965). English statesman and author; Prime Minister during World War II.

Cicero, Marcus Tullius (106–43 B.C.). Roman orator, philosopher, and man of letters.

Coleridge, Samuel Taylor (1772–1834). English romantic poet; author of "The Rime of the Ancient Mariner."

Congreve, William (1670–1729). English dramatist.

Conrad, Joseph (1857–1924). Polish-born English novelist.

Cooper, James Fenimore (1789–1851). American novelist; author of *The Leatherstocking Tales,* a series of five novels.

Dante (Alighieri) (1265–1321). Italian poet; author of the epic poem *The Divine Comedy*.

Defoe, Daniel (1660?–1731). English novelist; author of *Robinson Crusoe*.

Dickens, Charles (1812–1870). English novelist; author of *A Tale of Two Cities*.

Dickinson, Emily (1830–1886). American poet. Of the nearly 2,000 poems she wrote, only two were published in her lifetime.

Donne, John (1572?–1631). English poet and clergyman; chief exponent of the metaphysical style.

Dos Passos, John (1896–1970). American novelist.

Dostoevski, Feodor (1821–1881). Russian novelist.

Dowson, Ernest (1867–1900). English poet.

Doyle, Sir Arthur Conan (1859–1930). English physician, novelist, and short story writer; best known as the creator of Sherlock Holmes.

Dreiser, Theodore (1871–1945). American novelist.

Dumas, Alexandre (1802–1870). French novelist and dramatist; author of *The Three Musketeers*.

Eliot, T[homas] S[tearns] (1888–1965). American-born English poet, critic, and dramatist.

Emerson, Ralph Waldo (1803–1882). American poet and essayist.

Faulkner, William (1897–1962). American novelist and short story writer.

Field, Eugene (1850–1895). American poet and journalist; author of many popular and sentimental poems for children.

FitzGerald, Edward (1809–1883). English writer; translator of the poem *Rubáiyát of Omar Khayyám*.

Fitzgerald, F[rancis] Scott [Key] (1896–1940). American novelist and short story writer, known as the spokesman of the "Jazz Age;" author of *The Great Gatsby*.

Franklin, Benjamin (1706–1790). American author, statesman, inventor, printer, scientist; publisher of *Poor Richard's Almanac*. His autobiography is considered a classic.

Frost, Robert (1874–1963). American poet.

Gilbert, Sir William Schwenck (1836–1911). English satirist, dramatist, poet and librettist; best known for his work with Arthur Sullivan on the Gilbert and Sullivan (also known as the Savoy) operas.

Goethe, Johann Wolfgang von (1749–1832). German poet, playwright, and novelist; author of *Faust*.

Gray, Thomas (1716–1771). English poet; one of the forerunners of the romantic movement in England; author of "Elegy Written in a Country Churchyard."

Hardy, Thomas (1840–1928). English novelist and poet.

Hawthorne, Nathaniel (1804–1864). American novelist and short story writer.

Hemingway, Ernest (1899–1961). American novelist, short story writer, and journalist.

Henry, O. (pen name of William Sydney Porter) (1862–1910). American short story writer; famous for surprise endings.

Herbert, George (1593–1633). English poet of the metaphysical school.

Herodotus (c.480–c.425 B.C.). Greek historian, known as "the Father of History."

Herrick, Robert (1591–1674). English poet.

Heywood, John (1497?–1580?). English poet and epigrammist.

Homer (9th century B.C.?). Greek poet; generally presumed to be the author of the *Odyssey* and the *Iliad*.

Hungerford, M[argaret] W[olfe] (1855?–1897). Irish novelist; she wrote thirty books, most of which she signed "The Duchess." Author of *Molly Bawn*.

Johnson, Samuel, (1709–1784). Known as Dr. Johnson. English lexicographer and man of letters.

Juvenal, Decimus Junius (A.D. 60?–140?) Roman satirist.

Keats, John (1795–1821). English romantic poet.

Kipling, Rudyard (1865–1936). English novelist, short story writer, poet.

Lawrence, D.H. (1885–1930). English novelist, short story writer, poet, essayist. Author of *Lady Chatterley's Lover, Sons and Lovers,* and *Women in Love.*

Lewis, (Harry) Sinclair (1885–1951). American novelist.

Longfellow, Henry Wadsworth (1807–1882). American poet.

Lovelace, Richard (1618–1658). English poet.

Lyly, John (1554?–1606). English novelist and dramatist; author of *Euphues.*

Malory, Sir Thomas (15th century). English writer; author of *Le Morte d' Arthur.*

Marvell, Andrew (1621–1678). English poet.

Melville, Herman (1819–1891). American novelist, short story writer, poet. Best known for his classic novel *Moby Dick.*

Miller, Arthur (1915–). American playwright and novelist.

Milton, John (1608–1674). English poet and prose writer; author of the epic *Paradise Lost.*

Omár Khayyám (d.1123). Persian poet; author of the *Rubáiyát of Omár Khayyám.*

O'Neill, Eugene (1888–1953). American playwright.

Plutarch (A.D. c.46–c.120). Greek biographer, essayist, author of philosophical writings.

Poe, Edgar Allan (1809–1849). American poet, critic, short story writer. Perhaps best known for his tales of horror.

Pope, Alexander (1688–1744). English satirical poet.

Porter, Katherine Anne (1890–1980). American novelist and short story writer.

Quintilian (A.D. 35–c. 99). Roman rhetorician and teacher of oratory.

Roosevelt, Franklin Delano (1882–1945). Thirty-second president of the United States, from 1933 to 1945.

Scott, Sir Walter (1771–1832). Scottish novelist and poet.

Shaw, George Bernard (1856–1950). Irish dramatist.

Shelley, Percy Bysshe (1792–1822). English romantic poet.

Steinbeck, John (1902–1968). American novelist and short story writer.

Stevenson, Robert Louis (1850–1894). Scottish novelist, poet, historian and biographer.

Stowe, Harriet Beecher (1811–1896). American novelist; author of *Uncle Tom's Cabin*.

Swift, Jonathan (1667–1745). English satirist, poet, and political writer.

Tennyson, Alfred (1809–1892). Referred to as Alfred, Lord Tennyson. English poet.

Thackeray, William Makepeace (1811–1863). English novelist and satirist; author of *Vanity Fair.*

Thomas, Dylan (1914–1953). Welsh poet and prose writer.

Thoreau, Henry David (1817–1862). American essayist, naturalist, poet; author of *Walden.*

Tolstoy, Leo (1828–1910). Russian novelist; author of *War and Peace.*

Virgil, (or Vergil) (70–19 B.C.) Roman poet; author of *The Aeneid.*

Wilde, Oscar (1854–1900). Irish poet, dramatist, novelist.

Williams Tennessee (pen name of Thomas Lanier Williams) (1914–). American playwright; author of *A Streetcar Named Desire.*

Wolfe, Thomas (1900–1938). American novelist.

Wordsworth, William (1770–1850). English romantic poet.

Yeats, William Butler (1865–1939). Irish poet and dramatist.

Bibliography

Asimov, Isaac. *Asimov's Guide to Shakespeare.* Garden City, N.Y.: Doubleday & Co., Inc., 1970.

Bartlett, John. *Bartlett's Familiar Quotations,* 14th ed., edited by Emily Morison Beck. Boston and Toronto: Little, Brown and Company, 1968.

Baugh, Albert, C., ed. *A Literary History of England.* New York: Appleton-Century-Crofts, Inc., 1948.

Benét, William Rose, ed. *The Reader's Encyclopedia,* 2nd ed. New York: Thomas Y. Crowell, 1965.

The Bible, King James Version.

Brewer, E. Cobham. *Brewer's Dictionary of Phrase and Fable,* edited by Ivor H. Evans. New York and Evanston, Ill.: Harper & Row, 1971.

Burnam, Tom. *The Dictionary of Misinformation.* New York: Thomas Y. Crowell, 1975.

Campbell, Oscar James, and Edward G. Quinn, eds. *The Reader's Encyclopedia of Shakespeare.* New York: Thomas Y. Crowell, 1966.

Carroll, Lewis (Charles Lutwidge Dodgson). *The Annotated Alice,* introduction and notes by Martin Gardner. Cleveland, Ohio, and New York: World Publishing Co., 1960.

The Encyclopedia Americana. Danbury, Conn.: Americana Corporation, 1978.

Hyman, Robin, ed. *The Quotation Dictionary.* New York: The Macmillan Company, 1962.

Miller, Madeleine S. and J. Lane. *Harper's Bible Dictionary.* New York, Evanston, Ill., and London: Harper & Row, 1961.

The Oxford Dictionary of Quotations, 2nd ed., introduction by Bernard Darwin. London: Oxford University Press, 1955.

Roberts, Kate Louise, ed. *Hoyt's New Cyclopedia of Practical Quotations.* New York and London: Funk and Wagnalls Company, 1940.

Stevenson, Burton, selecter and arranger. *The Macmillan Book of Proverbs, Maxims, and Famous Phrases.* New York: The Macmillan Company, 1968.

Trevelyan, George Macaulay. *History of England,* 3rd ed. London: Longmans, Green and Co. Ltd., 1945.

Webster's New Twentieth Century Dictionary of the English Language, 2nd ed., edited by Jean L. McKechnie. Cleveland, Ohio and New York: The World Publishing Company, 1962.